GRAN CANARIA

Travel with Marco Polo Insider Tips

INSIDER TIP Your shortcut to a great experience

MARCO POLO TOP HIGHLIGHTS

CATHEDRAL & PLAZA DE SANTA ANA ⭐

A leisurely journey through time: colonial palaces and palms around the plaza take you back 500 years (photo).

📷 *Tip: by the afternoon, the Old Town is cast in shade, so get there early to take the best photographs in the bright morning light.*

➤ p. 42, Las Palmas

ACUARIO POEMA DEL MAR ⭐

Sharks glide overhead and alongside you at the "Ocean Poem", Europe's biggest aquarium.

➤ p. 46, Las Palmas

EL CARNAVAL ⭐

Salsa, samba and a spectacular festival – carnival on the Canaries is one of the best outside Brazil. See it for yourself, ideally in Las Palmas.

➤ p 18, Understand Gran Canaria

ARUCAS ⭐

Where there is water, money flows too! The magnificent "cathedral", exotic park and many architectural gems attest to the wealth of Arucas.

➤ p. 64, The North

MUSEO Y PARQUE ARQUEOLÓGICO CUEVA PINTADA ⭐

Back to the roots: the archaeological park around the "Painted Cave" *(Cueva Pintada)* brings to life the world of Gran Canaria's indigenous people.

➤ p. 69, The North

TEROR ⭐

Teror, home of the Virgin of the Pine, is a major pilgrimage site with a majestic church.

📷 *Tip: using a zoom lens to photograph the "Street of the Balconies" will make it look like a piece of abstract art.*

➤ p. 62, The North

TEJEDA ⭐

Tejeda has been officially named "one of Spain's most beautiful villages". The mountain panorama is breathtaking!

📷 *Tip: avoid visiting around midday, not just because of the hazy light but the crowds too.*

➤ p. 83, The Centre

PICO DE LAS NIEVES ⭐

At 2,000m, the "Snowy Peak" offers the best views of the entire island!

📷 *Tip: the most spectacular photographs can be taken in the afternoon when the trade wind clouds create a mystical atmosphere.*

➤ p. 83, The Centre

PUERTO DE MOGÁN ⭐

Great resort architecture: jetties and bridges by the water, secluded squares, and boats moored by your front door create a Venetian flair.

➤ p. 112, The South Coast

DUNAS DE MASPALOMAS ⭐

Sahara feeling: among the waves of sand you will feel like Lawrence of Arabia.

📷 *Tip: the dunes look their very best in the gentle light of the setting sun.*

➤ p. 103, The South Coast

CONTENTS

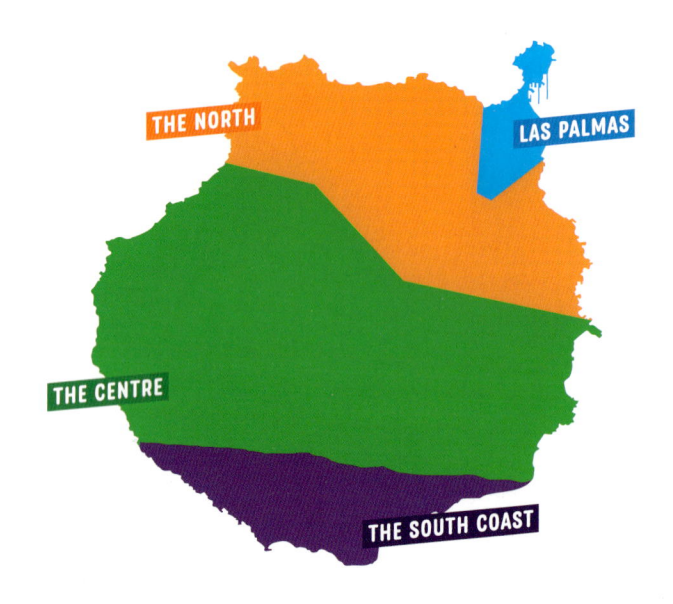

36	**REGIONAL OVERVIEW**
38	**LAS PALMAS**
54	**THE NORTH**
Telde & around	58
Santa Brígida & around	60
Vega de San Mateo	61
Teror	62
Arucas & around	64
Santa María de Guía & around	66
Gáldar & around	68
Puerto de las Nieves & around	70
72	**THE CENTRE**
Mogán & around	76
La Aldea de San Nicolás & around	78
Artenara & around	79
Cruz de Tejeda & around	82
Tejeda & around	83
Ayacata & around	85
San Bartolomé de Tirajana & around	87
Santa Lucía & around	88
Agüimes & around	90
92	**THE SOUTH COAST**
San Agustín & around	96
Playa del Inglés & around	98
Maspalomas & around	103
Meloneras	106
Arguineguín & around	108
Puerto Rico & around	110
Puerto de Mogán & around	112

CONTENTS

MARCO POLO HIGHLIGHTS
2 Top 10 highlights

BEST OF GRAN CANARIA
8 ...when it rains
9 ... on a budget
10 ... with children
11 ... classic experiences

GET TO KNOW GRAN CANARIA
14 Discover Gran Canaria
17 At a glance
18 Understand Gran Canaria
21 True or false?

EATING, SHOPPING, SPORT
26 Eating & drinking
30 Shopping
32 Sport & activities

MARCO POLO REGIONS
36 Regional overview

DISCOVERY TOURS
116 In the shadow of the "Snowy Peak"
122 Through the wild *cumbre*
128 A day in the green north

GOOD TO KNOW

132 **HOLIDAY BASICS**
Arrival, Getting around, Emergencies, Essentials, Festivals & events, Weather

140 **WORDS & PHRASES IN SPANISH**
Don't be lost for words

142 **HOLIDAY VIBES**
Books, films, music & blogs

144 **TRAVEL PURSUIT**
The Marco Polo holiday quiz

146 **INDEX & CREDITS**

148 **DOS & DON'TS**
How to avoid slip-ups & blunders

⊙ Plan your visit	🍴 Eating/drinking	☂ Rainy day activities
€-€€€ Price categories	🛍 Shopping	🐷 Budget activities
(*) Premium-rate phone number	🍸 Going out	👪 Family activities
	⛱ Top beaches	▶ Classic experiences

(📖 A2) Refers to the removable pull-out map
(0) Located off the map

BEST OF GRAN CANARIA

Dunas de Maspalomas

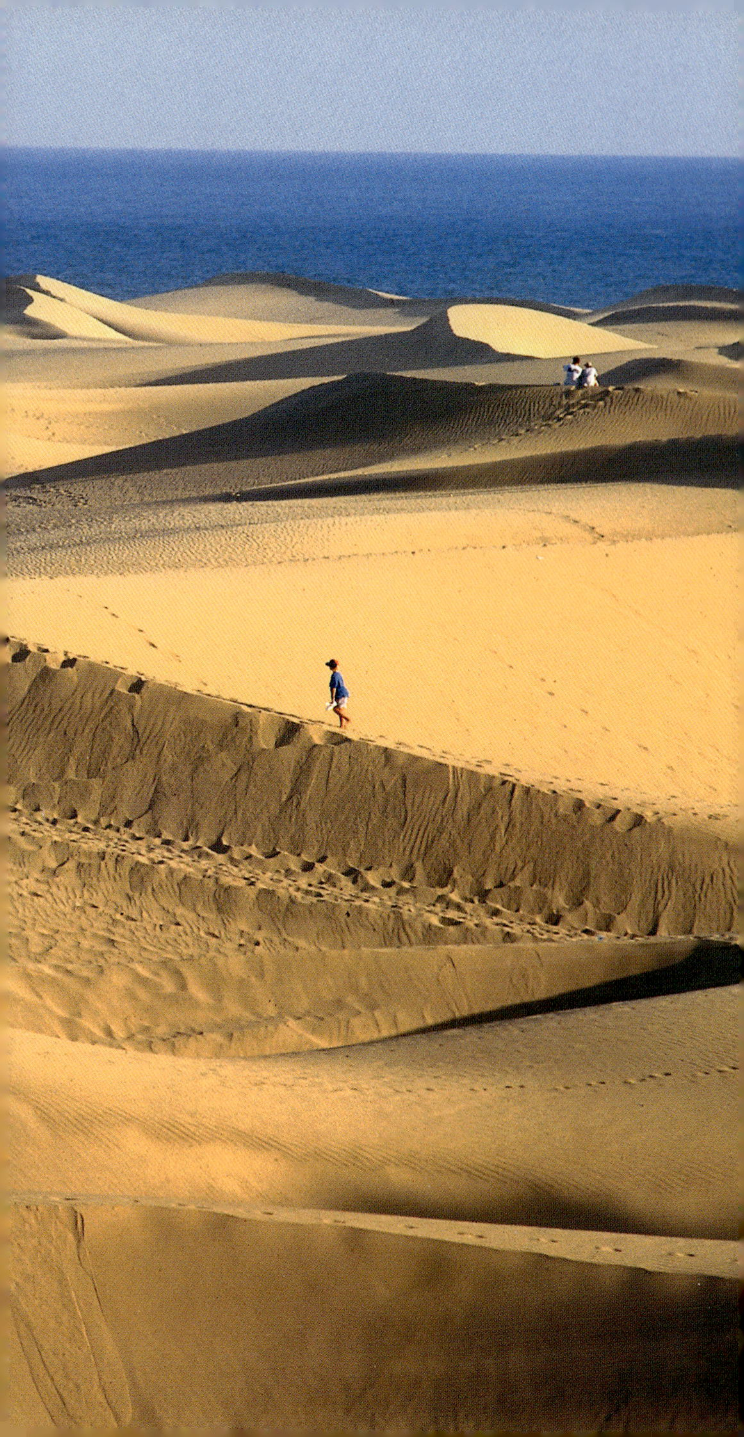

BEST WHEN IT RAINS

ACTIVITIES TO BRIGHTEN YOUR DAY

BATTLE OF THE BIG BOYS
Join Canarios of all age groups and cheer on the heavyweight stars – men and women – at the *Terreros de la Lucha Canaria*. To win, competitors must throw their opponents to the ground.
➤ p. 21, Understand Gran Canaria

EVERYTHING UNDER ONE ROOF
In Las Palmas's two main shopping malls – *CC Las Arenas* and *CC El Muelle* – there are countless trendy shops as well as cinemas showing the latest blockbusters (photo).
➤ p. 30, Shopping

WORLD OF THE GUANCHES
Even if museums aren't usually your thing, you will love the *Museo Canario*. It's the perfect place to discover the world of the island's indigenous people.
➤ p. 44, Las Palmas

TAKE REFUGE IN THE BASILICA
When it rains, the gargoyles of Teror's *Basílica de Nuestra Señora del Pino* "spit" at passers-by. You're better off seeking shelter inside, where you can admire the richly decorated statue of the Madonna.
➤ p. 63, The North

RELAXATION ON TAP
From Ayurveda to Zen, *Talasoterapia Canarias* pampers you, body and soul. And if you want a massage, the hydro-jets in the 36°C saltwater pool will do the trick.
➤ p. 112, The South Coast

GO UNDER WATER
If it rains, head underwater! *Submarine Adventure* leaves Puerto de Mogán and descends to the seabed where you can watch trumpet fish swimming around a shipwreck.
➤ p. 114, The South Coast

BEST ON A BUDGET

FOR SMALLER WALLETS

SCUBA DIVING TASTER
If you are uncertain as to whether you like the underwater world, why not try it out? Almost all diving schools offer free pool sessions!
➤ p. 33, Sport & activities

UPLIFTING EXPERIENCE
You can witness Spanish piety during mass in Las Palmas's *Catedral de Santa Ana*. It's an impressive experience and admission is free during church services.
➤ p. 42, Las Palmas

FREE TICKET TO THE ART SCENE
Experimental art, provocative art and curious art: exhibitions, as well as lectures and concerts, are held for free at the *Centro Atlántico de Arte Moderno (CAAM)*.
➤ p. 43, Las Palmas

FOLKLORE LIVE
The perfect spots to experience Canarian folk music are the *Parque de Santa Catalina* on Saturdays (from 11am) and the *Pueblo Canario* on Sundays (from 11.30am), when enthusiastic singers, musicians and dancers demonstrate their skills – all wearing traditional costumes.
➤ p. 45 & p.46, Las Palmas

RUM TASTING
On a guided tour of the *Arehucas* distillery (photo), Europe's biggest producer of rum, you can admire their countless oak casks and taste their exquisite rum and liquors.
➤ p. 65, The North

TAKE A BREAK UNDER PINE TREES
Canarios love to picnic in the forest by the *Cueva de las Niñas* reservoir, where rustic tables, benches, barbecues and water taps are provided.
➤ p. 86, The Centre

BEST WITH CHILDREN

FUN FOR YOUNG AND OLD

SEAHORSES & BASKING SHARKS
In the enormous *Poema del Mar* aquarium, ocean dwellers float just above your head and you can get right up close to the sharks, moray eels and parrot fish. Watch colourful corals, tiger fish, piranhas and crocodiles, then walk across to the pier where historic sailing ships sometimes moor.
➤ p. 46, Las Palmas

CAMEL RIDE THROUGH THE MINI SAHARA
Camel Safari at the Charco de Maspalomas and *Camel Safari Park La Baranda* near Arteara both offer camel-riding expeditions that last about half an hour. In Arteara they also breed the camels.
➤ p. 88, The Centre and p. 104, The South Coast

DIVE IN
If you want more than the Atlantic Ocean or the surf is too big, *Aqualand* in Maspalomas offers water slides, wave pools and man-made rivers.
➤ p. 104, The South Coast

MEET THE ANIMALS
Although admission to *Palmitos Park* (photo) is not exactly cheap, the children will be in heaven: dolphin and parrot shows, monkeys, meerkats and reptiles, exotic birds and butterflies as well as an aquarium with many tropical fish.
➤ p. 105, The South Coast

ANGRY BIRDS
Inspired by the popular video game, the *Angry Birds Activity Park* in Puerto Rico features scooter ramps and bag jumps, bouncy castles and climbing walls.
➤ p. 111, The South Coast

BEST 🚩
CLASSIC EXPERIENCES

ONLY ON GRAN CANARIA

NOT ONLY FOR BOTANISTS
The 2,000 different plants that grow in the *Jardín Canario* can be found nowhere else on earth! You'll see dragon trees, spurge and dazzling red campanulas that are threatened by extinction.
➤ p. 53, Las Palmas

FLOWERY CHEESE
Queso de flor, the most unusual Canarian dairy product, tastes especially good accompanied by a glass of red wine at the *Tienda de Arturo* in Santa María de Guía.
➤ p. 67, The North

WEST COAST SUNSETS
Every evening, the beach promenades of *Puerto de la Aldea de San Nicolas* and *Puerto de las Nieves* (photo) become the stage for one of nature's greatest spectacles!
➤ p. 70, The North, p. 78, The Centre

VIRGIN OF THE ROCK
There are thousands of caves on Gran Canaria and in Artenara you can find a spectacular example in the *Virgen de la Cuevita* chapel. Next to it is the *Museo de las Casas Cuevas*.
➤ p. 79 & p. 80, The Centre

RESERVOIRS
The reservoirs are like a string of pearls in the mountain landscape. Especially idyllic after rainfall in winter is the *Embalse de Soria*.
➤ p. 86, The Centre

FRESH FISH
Fish always tastes best not far from where it was caught, with a fresh sea breeze and the tang of salt in the air. Try the *Bar Playa El Boya* in Arguineguín.
➤ p. 109, The South Coast

GET TO KNOW GRAN CANARIA

Anything goes at the Las Palmas carnival!

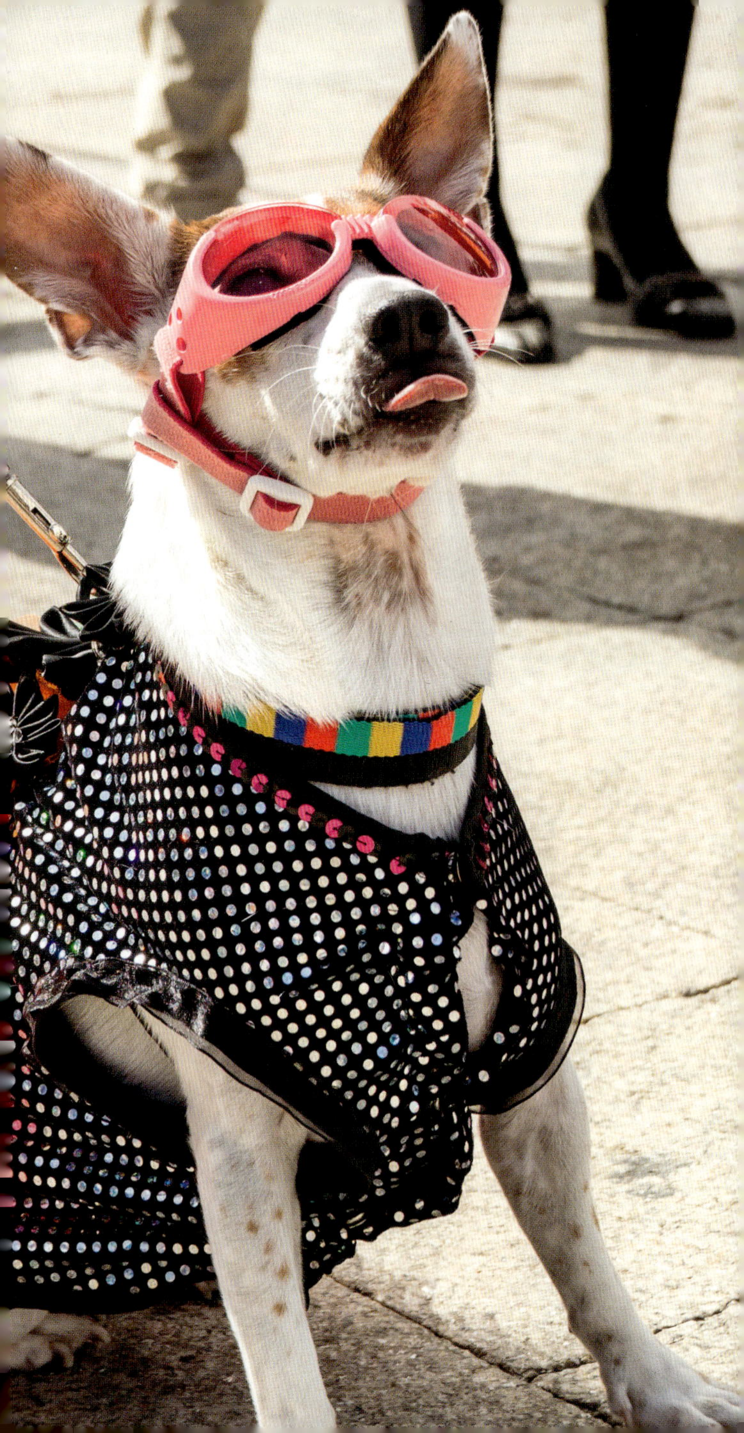

DISCOVER GRAN CANARIA

Gran Canaria's landscape is characterised by *barrancos* and mountain ridges

It's the same picture every morning: men armed with machetes working on the banana plantations, fishermen setting out to sea in their boats, shepherds taking their flocks up to higher pastures. Life follows a relaxed pace in most of the island's mountain villages. The capital, Las Palmas, seems light years away.

FACELIFT FOR THE HOTELS

Similarly far removed are the resorts in the south, which welcome more than four million visitors a year. An armada of people – from the 24-hour taxi drivers and cleaners to the lifeguards in their watchtowers – take care of the holidaymaker's every wish.

500 BCE
Berber people from northwest Africa settle on the archipelago

1st century CE
Pliny the Elder describes the "Canaria" group of islands in his "Historia Naturalis"

1478-83
The indigenous Canarians are conquered by the Spanish

1492
Columbus stops over at Gran Canaria

16th to 17th centuries
The Canaries become Spain's first ever colony

1936-1939
The Spanish Civil War, which begins on the Canaries, heralds Franco's dictatorship

GET TO KNOW GRAN CANARIA

Of course, there are still some ugly hotel buildings and a few run-down shopping centres, but over the past few years efforts have been made to spruce up the island's image. Quite a few hotels have been revamped, while the new resorts of Meloneras and Playa de Amadores have hotels that resemble castles or African citadels. Visitors will find everything that is in fashion today, from golf courses, Asian-inspired spa oases and yoga workshops to pilates and Nordic walking on the beach. Gran Canaria caters to all tastes, whether you are looking for the all-inclusive packages in the resorts, or want to head for mountains, stay at a finca and hike along restored trails, relax in one of the coastal villages or live it up in Las Palmas.

SPANIARDS AGAINST INDIGENOUS CANARIANS

Hardly a trace remains of what Las Palmas would have looked like on 24 June, 1478, when the Spanish conquistador Juan Rejón landed on the island with his 600 followers, to claim the third largest Canarian island for the Castilian crown. For five years the indigenous Guanche people struggled to fight off the conquerors, but, with their modern weapons, the Spaniards were ultimately successful. They completely "remodelled" the island by clearing the laurel and pine forests to make way for sugar cane and later grapes for wine. Enslaved native Canarians and Africans toiled on these new plantations. Shipping trade between Europe and America made the city elite wealthy; the rest of the island was impoverished, prompting many islanders to emigrate to America.

Since 1950 Chartered flights begin to bring large numbers of tourists

1975 After Franco's death, Spain becomes a democratic country

1986 Spain becomes a member of both the EU and NATO

2010–2017 Global economic crisis: the construction industry collapses with many people losing their job and home

Since 2018 With the Canaries again being regarded as "safe", tourism experiences a new boom

2019 Forest fires destroy thousands of acres of land

ENDLESS TOURISM

The island only really started to flourish with the arrival of tourism. Its rapid development into one of the largest holiday resorts in Europe started in the south in the early 1960s. Hotel complexes and resorts for more than 100,000 guests sprang up between San Agustín and Puerto de Mogán and the expansion continues, with no end in sight. The beaches and dunes are simply too inviting, the good weather too stable and the location between the mountains and sea too perfect. However, many tourists are shocked at how barren the south of the island is when they arrive at the airport in Gando. But fear not: Gran Canaria is an island with a wide variety of fauna and flora.

CONTRASTING NORTH & SOUTH

Gran Canaria is almost circular in shape, and the 1,949-m-high Pico de las Nieves, the highest point in the *cumbre* (the central mountainous region) is almost exactly in the middle. From here, valleys formed by erosion branch out to the coast. *Calderas* (bowl-shaped craters) are a reminder of the island's volcanic origins. Parched by the sun in the south and often feeling subtropical in the north, the enchanting island has dream beaches, dunes and an unspoilt mountain wilderness. No other Canary Island is as rugged and furrowed with *barrancos* (ravines) as Gran Canaria. In the north, the lower mountain slopes are covered by forest. Lizards rustle through the undergrowth, birds of prey circle overhead and the canary – in its original form – swirls through the woods as a yellow and green serin.

FROM BIG CITY FLAIR TO EXPERIENCING NATURE

However, there is more to Gran Canaria then contrasting landscapes: as well as the big city bustle of Las Palmas, you'll find pretty villages and small towns where the pace of life is much slower. Artenara, for example, is a perfectly preserved cave town, while Teror, with its antique basilica, cobbled streets and façades with wooden balconies, is regarded as a prime example of Canarian architecture. Experience the colourful carnival with its joyful parades; taste Canarian cuisine and enjoy the island's pleasant wine; go scuba diving, hiking, swimming or windsurfing; party all night or just relax: you will not be bored on Gran Canaria.

GET TO KNOW GRAN CANARIA

AT A GLANCE

850,000 inhabitants

London: 9 million

1,560KM² area

UK: 242,500km²

236km of coastline

UK coastline: 12,400km

While it is only **200km** to Africa, the Spanish mainland is almost 1,300km away

46% of the island's landmass is protected

HIGHEST PEAK: PICO DE LAS NIEVES

1,949M

There is a viewing platform just below the peak

MOST POPULAR MONTH FOR TRAVELLING

DECEMBER

LAS PALMAS
capital with approx. 400,000 residents
Liverpool: 500,000

300,000 PEOPLE join the Gran Cabalgata, the annual carnival parade

GÁLDAR AND TELDE WERE THE TWO MAIN TOWNS OF THE INDIGENOUS CANARIANS

UNDERSTAND GRAN CANARIA

THE INDIGENOUS CANARIANS

Many Canarians have Berber names such as Yeray and Yaiza, Guayarmina and Bentejuí. Long-forgotten ancient sites are being excavated and restored and archaeological finds put on display in modern museums. It's really only a recent development that is bringing the original people into the focus of today's Canarians. The Spanish conquistadors who subjugated the island's inhabitants in 1483 considered them to be "heretics" and "savages" who – as they saw it – had to be tamed and forced to accept the correct religious belief. Their language and culture were quickly lost. Even in the 20th century – during the long period of the Franco dictatorship – associating with the "inferior" indigenous inhabitants was considered taboo. As Canarian archaeology is still in its infancy, many questions have not been answered. It is assumed that the indigenous Guanche people descended from Berber tribes in northwest Africa and came to the island from the fifth century BCE. But precisely how they arrived and why they had no contact with their neighbouring islands remains a mystery. What we do know is that they ate fish: they fished with their bare hands or using the milky latex of the *Euphorbia ingens* (the "candelabra tree") which is poisonous and anaesthetises the fish. The original Canarians were mainly farmers who tended sheep and goats and cultivated barley, which they used to make *gofio* flour, their staple food.

FIESTA DE LA FIESTA

Preparations for ★ *El Carnaval* go on for months: *carrozas* (floats) are constructed and decorated, costumes made, masks and disguises assembled. Every village has its *murgas*, costumed groups of clowns who parade through the streets singing and dancing during the *desfiles* (parades). The fun usually begins in the evening and continues all through the night. The coronation of the *Reina del Carnaval* (Carnival Queen) is shown live on television across Spain (and the costumes of the contestants often cost as much as a middle-of-the-range car). Each carnival day ends with a *mogollón*, dancing to Latin rhythms

GET TO KNOW GRAN CANARIA

until the early hours of the morning. The *entierro de la sardina* – burial of the sardine – is the magnificent end to all the celebrations. Nobody really knows why a fish is carried to its grave. The final procession of black-clad mourners accompanied by a massive cardboard sardine culminates in a display of illuminated arches, rockets and fireworks.

DRAGON OF THE CANARIANS

The Guanches considered it sacred and drank its blood for its healing properties. It also impressed the first explorers, who siphoned off its blood to sell on Europe's markets. It was even used to stain violins! But allow us to reveal the secret: the Canarian dragon (*el drago* in Spanish, *Dracaena drago* in Latin) is a tree, not an animal. With its crown of lance-shaped leaves and a little imagination, it could indeed resemble a dragon. In any case, it is an impressive sight! Its closest relatives live in Africa and Asia but, as a result of the island's isolated location, the Canarian "dragon" has developed a number of unique features. Gran Canaria has its own subspecies that is not found anywhere else in the world. The plant was named *Dracaena tamaranae* after the island's pre-Hispanic name, "Tamarán".

CAMELS

The one-humped dromedaries probably arrived on Gran Canaria with the first Europeans in the early 15th century and were used as work animals. Although their careers had come to an end with the introduction of machinery, camels have experienced a renaissance thanks to tourism. There are two stations on the island where you can ride the camels every day, one in Maspalomas and another in Arteara. Dromedaries are bred in Arteara where you can see young animals at close quarters.

Months of hard work go into the preparations for El Carnaval, the highlight of the year

WIND-BLOWN WANDERERS

In the south of the island the shimmering sand dunes reach heights of up to 12m. Measuring 1.5km at their widest point, they spread inland over an area of 418 hectares: the protected *Dunas de Maspalomas*. Seen against the blue of the sea, they make a delightful picture (used in every advertisement for the island). Although people often assume that they were created by Saharan sand blown across from Africa, they are actually formed by corals and shells that were ground by the waves and washed ashore. And they move – albeit at a snail's pace – between 2m and 5m a year towards the west, and are continuously reshaped by the trade winds. This movement is only stopped by the increase in vegetation and the weakening winds further inland.

DONKEY'S STOMACH

"Panza del burro!" (donkey's stomach) is what the Canarios call the clouds blown in by the trade winds that gather and build dense formations in the north of the island. The origin of this name is rather curious. Many of the locals' ancestors were farmers and, back in the day, almost all of them had a donkey that was used as a draught and pack animal. When it became hot at midday and siesta time approached, farmers used to lie down beneath their donkeys to get some shade. Looking up, they only saw the animal's white and grey stomach, the same colour as the trade wind clouds and hanging just as low!

BETTER LIVING

Gran Canaria is as "holey" as Swiss cheese – the holes being caves in its volcanic rock. And why build houses if

Camel riding in the Maspalomas dunes

GET TO KNOW GRAN CANARIA

Cave houses are traditional in the Guayadeque gorge

you have caves? The Guanches lived in them, stored their food supplies in them and buried their dead in them. Little has changed in the past 1,000 years and many people still live in caves today. The caves are warm in winter and cool in summer and, if you dig your house out of the rock, you're not blotting the landscape with ugly new buildings. Most of the cave villages are in the central hills in Artenara and Acusa as well as in Barranco de Guayadeque in the east. You can even stay in some of them.

ANCIENT WRESTLING

Lucha Canaria was already popular in the days of the first Canarios. Twelve fighters from two teams wrestle in pairs against each other in a ring approximately 15m in diameter and covered with sawdust or sand. The *luchadores* use a variety of wrestling holds to get the better of their opponent and throw him to the ground in a maximum three-minute bout. It's not only down to weight, but also technique and speed. There are 🚩 *Terreros de la Lucha Canaria*, wrestling arenas, in Puerto de Mogán, Ingenio, Gáldar, Firgas and Las Palmas. Tourist information offices have details of forthcoming fights.

SNOW IN THE ETERNAL SPRING

Snow falls every two or three years in Gran Canaria's *cumbre*, the rugged mountainous regions around the

This is no fight over a deckchair, but training for an upcoming wrestling match

1,949-m-high Pico de las Nieves. And whenever it happens it makes headlines in the newspapers and local television channels send teams of reporters into the mountains. At the weekend, thousands of Canarios set out to have snowball fights, build snowmen and queue for a cup of hot chocolate at one of the pop-up stalls.

WATER FROM THE SEA

All 850,000 inhabitants and over four million visitors want to drink, shower, wash their laundry and swim in the pool. Then there are the terraced fields, banana and tomato plantations, golf courses and gardens, as well as some industry. Imagine how much water all that requires! And it's a well-known fact that it doesn't rain much on sunny islands; in fact, there's a chronic water shortage. There used to be rivers on Gran Canaria, and dense bay forests drew moisture from the trade wind clouds, while the farmers used wells. Now, the trees have been cut down, the wells have dried up and there is only one small stream on the island. Rainwater is collected in gigantic reservoirs that often appear to be ominously empty. Instead of digging ever deeper into the ground to tap the meagre groundwater supply through mile-long galleries, Gran Canaria opted to make use of an inexhaustible resource: the ocean. The island would not be what it is today without water, and you probably wouldn't be visiting Gran Canaria either. The engineering skill lies in extracting the salt from the seawater. Initially this was done with expensive oil-powered systems, but today environmentally friendly osmosis is used. As usual, though, it costs money and energy – so please DO NOT waste water!

GET TO KNOW GRAN CANARIA

WHAT A PEAK

Many millions of years ago, a vast continent broke in two, and since then these two parts – America and Africa – have been drifting apart. Where there are breaks in the earth's crust below them, hot liquid magma makes its way up from the depths. It shoots through the surface with tremendous force, mixes with sea water that cools it down and turns it into rock. The result is the island's underwater plinth. Gradually the magna rises above the surface of the sea and cools down in the air: a new island is born! From this point onwards it is exposed to the elements: the surf nibbles away at its edges, thunderstorms and heavy rain leave their marks in the rocks. The most dramatic parts of Gran Canaria's landscape have been declared a UNESCO Biosphere Reserve.

WINE

The Spanish brought the first vines to the island where they thrived in the volcanic soil. Soon the wine made from the heady Malvasía grapes became very sought after. But, for a number of reasons, Canarian wine production decreased dramatically until Spain entered the EU and substantial subsidies were made available. The Canarios have now rediscovered their old wine: small family wineries have been modernised and new bodegas have opened. The grapes are harvested in September so that the young wine can be tasted along with freshly roasted chestnuts on St Martin's Day at the beginning of November. Watch out for the "venta de vino" signs (wine for sale)!

> **INSIDER TIP**
> **Make merry on St Martin's Day**

Vines in the Agaete Valley

EATING SHOPPING SPORT

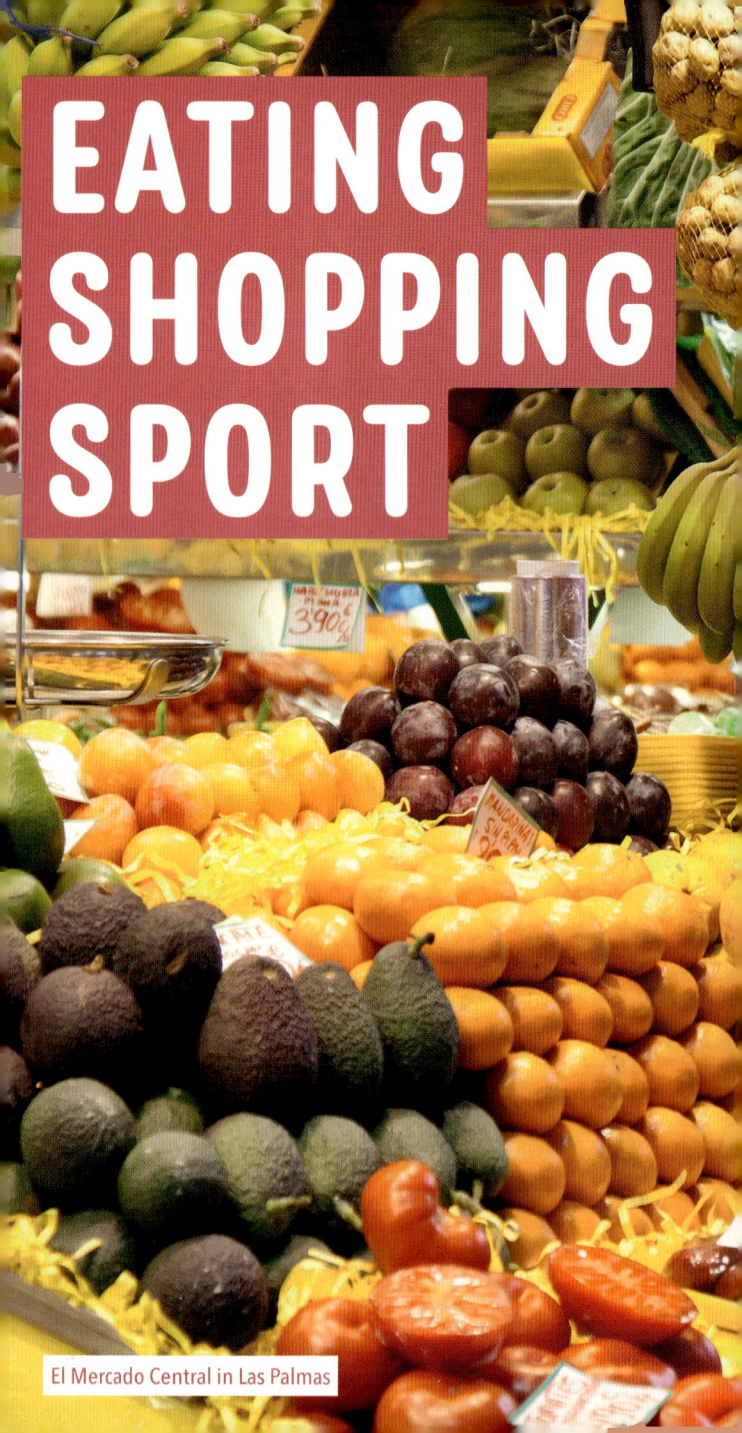

El Mercado Central in Las Palmas

PERAS
ERCOLINI
360

NARANJAS
0,75
€

EATING & DRINKING

Chef recommends: *potaje canario* – a hearty vegetable soup – and *gofio escaldado* – fish broth thickened with *gofio* flour. Accompany it with bread and a bottle of Firgas mineral water and *¡Buen provecho!* These traditional dishes seldom find their way onto the menus of tourist restaurants, which is a pity because they are the best way to get a feeling for real Canarian life.

GOFIO – WITH A ROASTED AROMA

The islanders themselves always cook simple dishes but with that extra something. The original Canarians used watermills in the mountains to grind roasted corn into flour that was stored in large sacks piled up against the walls. The result was a nondescript beige-coloured powder: *gofio*, the staple food of an entire people. Whether made of barley, wheat or corn, gofio flour was always available; it was rich in protein, very versatile and could be stored for a long time. It was baked into bread and tortillas, stirred into soups and sauces, and eaten along with fish and meat.

Today, *gofio* is experiencing something of a renaissance because it is more nutritious than meat, and rich in vitamin A and C as well as iron, magnesium and zinc.

STRAIGHT FROM THE POT & HOT OFF THE GRIDDLE

Stews and soups, combined with leftovers from other meals, still form the basis of the *cocina casera* – the Canarian home-style cooking that is popular in simple restaurants. One classic dish is *ropa vieja* ("old clothes") – leftovers as its name suggests. This thick stew of chickpeas, peppers, bits of meat

INSIDER TIP Delicious leftovers

Typically Canarian: *sancocho canario* (left) as well as *mojo rojo* and *mojo verde* (right)

==and thyme is a delicious combination of flavours.== Hearty dishes include vegetable or meat stews *(potaje/puchero)* and the sour-and-savoury cress soup *(potaje de berros)*.

Especially at lunchtime, between 1pm and 3pm, workers tuck into a cheap meal in their local restaurant. Refined presentation and sophisticated service are secondary. What matters is that it is quick, the white bread is fresh and the servings are generous. Fish is usually served *a la plancha*, i.e. grilled on a hot griddle. Whether it is *vieja* (parrot fish), *caballa* (mackerel), *sama* (brace) or *bonito* (a kind of tuna), you can be sure that Canarian fish and seafood is always freshly caught.

HOMEMADE FOOD

The *cocina casera* also reflects the time when the Canaries were at the crossroads of two worlds. Yams from Africa, sweet potatoes from South America and saffron from La Mancha are all found in modern Canarian dishes. Caribbean *arroz a la cubana* – rice with tomato sauce, fried banana and fried egg – is very popular in traditional restaurants, as are *carajacas*, a local dish prepared with liver.

Other traditional Canarian specialities include *cherne al cilantro* (grouper with fresh coriander) or *en escabeche* (in a spicy sauce), *conejo en salmorejo* (pan-fried rabbit in bay and wine marinade) and *baifito en adobo* (kid goat in garlic sauce). It's usually best to avoid the touristy restaurants serving mediocre *paella* and instead opt for good regional cooking.

MORNING RITUALS

In contrast to lunch, breakfast tends to be rather spartan. Many are content with a *café solo* (espresso) or *cortado* (with a little milk) and a *bocadillo* – a

Street café in Las Palmas

bread roll with ham or cheese – at the bar on their way to work. Only after a long night on the town is a more substantial breakfast on the agenda with churros dipped in hot chocolate.

DINNER NOT TOO EARLY

When tourists go to local restaurants in the evening, they often find themselves alone. While many people from the north of Europe dine sometime between 6pm and 8pm, the Spaniards prefer to have a *merienda* – a snack of a few tapas, for example – to tide them over until later. The Canarios usually sit down to eat dinner with their families at about 9pm or 10pm when the temperature is more pleasant.

PALATABLE WINE & HEARTY CHEESE

The royal families of Europe used to be fond of wines from Gran Canaria and although these wines have seen a resurgence recently, wine from the Spanish mainland continues to dominate the market on the island. Only the *Denominación de Origen* (protected designation of origin) label guarantees that exclusively local grapes have been used to produce a particular product.

There are countless varieties of Canarian cheeses and they all go well with a glass of wine. The cheese is made from unpasteurised goat's, sheep's or cow's milk – or a mixture of all three – and is characterised by three levels of ripeness: *tierno* (fresh, mild), *semicurado* (semimature) and *curado* (mature). *Queso de flor* is utterly unique: the addition of thistle juice makes this the most unusual cheese on the Canaries. It's no surprise, then, that Canarios are among the biggest cheese lovers in Spain.

EATING & DRINKING

Today's Specials

Starters

CALDO DE PESCADO
Light fish soup with potatoes and herbs

GAMBAS AL AJILLO
Prawns in sizzling olive oil, spiced with garlic and chilli

RANCHO CANARIO
Hearty stew with chickpeas, pork, chorizo and noodles

Mains

CHERNE AL CILANTRO
Grouper fish with fresh coriander

SANCOCHO CANARIO
Saltfish stew served with vegetables and sweet potatoes

CONEJO AL SALMOREJO
Pan-fried rabbit, marinated in bay leaves, garlic and wine

CARNE DE CABRA/BAIFO EN ADOBO
Goat in a spicy sauce

Side dishes

MOJO ROJO
Spicy sauce made with chillies, oil, garlic, vinegar and salt

MOJO VERDE
A milder version with fresh coriander

PAPAS ARRUGADAS
Potatoes boiled in brine whose skin has begun to wrinkle (*arrugado* in Spanish) served with mojo rojo or verde

GOFIO ESCALDADO
Fish broth thickened with roasted gofio flour

Desserts

LECHE ASADA
A thick custard made of eggs, lemon zest, cinnamon and sugar

BIENMESABE
Thick golden-brown dessert made of honey, almonds, egg yolks and lemons (its name means "I like the taste of it")

FLAN CASERO
Home-made set caramel custard

SHOPPING

From shopping outlets to luxury boutiques, and from corner shops to farmers' markets, the Canarians love to shop, and there's plenty on offer. And if you suddenly realise at the airport that you've forgotten a souvenir, relax! There are shops selling Canarian goodies after you have checked in.

SHOPPING CENTRES

The best place to shop is in the capital, Las Palmas. On your way there, stop at one of Spain's largest and most beautifully located outlet stores: *Centro Comercial Las Terrazas* is right by the sea in Jinámar! There are two more attractive shopping centres in the beach and port districts of Las Palmas: *CC El Muelle* and *CC Las Arenas* have all the top international brands as well as cinemas, bistros, cafés and fast-food restaurants.

ARTS & CRAFTS

The craftpeople of Ingenio specialise in creating charmingly simple bags, hats, mats and bread baskets all intricately woven from the fronds of the Canarian date palm.

Pottery also has a long tradition on the Canaries. Rustic ware such as jugs, vases, pots, carafes and bowls is made for everyday use. *FEDAC (fedac.org)* is a state-run shop that promotes local arts and crafts. The quality is exceptional and the designs often unique. There are FEDAC branches in Las Palmas (Triana) and Playa del Inglés.

HOT FASHION

The island's government supports designers to promote Gran Canarian fashion labels, such as *Moda Cálida*. The slogan is *hecho en Canarias*, i.e. made on the Canaries. Other established labels include *Lenita-XLT* for

Traditional crafts (left) and modern accessories (right)

swimwear and *Las Afortunadas* for fun accessories.

Several events showcase Moda Cálida, including the *Fashion & Friends* lifestyle market in November and the *Swimwear Fashion Week* in June *(grancanariamodacalida.es)*.

SWEETS

Turrón, a nougat-like delicacy, is sold from roadside stands in and near the town of Teror. *Ron con miel*, honey rum from Arucas, is a sweet souvenir. Excellent *bienmesabe*, the delicious Canarian dessert made with honey and almonds, can be bought in supermarkets (*Tejeda* brand).

INDOOR & OUTDOOR MARKETS

Market stands are set up once a week in many villages. The largest market hall in Las Palmas is El Mercado Central in the Catalina district near the beach, with two floors of the freshest produce imaginable: stacks of avocados, papayas and mangos, artichokes and yams, small and large potatoes, herbs and spices.

INSIDER TIP *Fruit galore*

The other two market halls in the capital also offer a wonderful selection.

SPORT & ACTIVITIES

It's hard to think of a sport that isn't practised on Gran Canaria! Naturally, there is every type of water sport, but the Canarios also enjoy cycling, hiking, climbing and hang-gliding.

CYCLING

The island's geography and the variation in climate mean that you need to be in good physical shape if you want to tackle any of the more strenuous cycling tours. The Barranco de Ayagaures, the Barranco de Arguineguín, and higher up near the Cueva de las Niñas reservoir are just three of the many superb routes for road cyclists. But remember: you have to wear a helmet! Bikes can be rented from *Bike10Mil (Av. de Gran Canaria 30 | tel. 663 53 50 38 | bike10mil.com)* in Playa del Inglés; they also offers tours ranging from easy to difficult. *Free Motion (tel. 928 77 74 79 | free-motion.com)* has bike stations in Playa del Inglés (Hotel Sandy Beach) and Puerto de Mogán (Hotel Cordial Mogán Playa). You can even combine cycling with learning Spanish and/or wine tasting? Away from the holiday centres, *Villa del Monte (C/ Castaño Bajo 9 | tel. 928 64 43 89 | canary-bike.com)* in Santa Brígida is a meeting place for cyclists with bikes to hire and a workshop.

In Las Palmas you'll find well-maintained mountain and e-bikes (as well as motor scooters) at the *Las Palmas Bike Station (C/ 29 de Abril 63 | tel. 928 93 54 11, mobile tel. 605 06 10 24 | rental-bike-station-gran-canaria.com)*. They also offer professional guided tours with a Hike & Bike shuttle service. A minibus takes you into the mountains so that you can enjoy the exciting off-road descent back towards the coast.

> **INSIDER TIP**
> High above the city

You need to be fit to cycle on Gran Canaria

DIVING & SNORKELLING

The waters around Gran Canaria have a great variety of fish and fascinating underwater fauna. While snorkellers will be able to see small fish close to the shore, divers – with professionals accompanying them – will come face to face with tuna and barracudas further out. 🐷 Many diving schools offer free taster sessions in the pool!

The diving school *Náutico (6 dives 180 euros | IFA Interclub Atlantic | C/ Los Jazmines 2 | tel. 620 94 77 53 | divingcenter-nautico.com)* in San Agustín, offers courses ranging from beginners to instructor certification. You can book PADI courses and excursions to wrecks, reefs and caves, as well as night dives with *Top-Diving (5-dive package 180 euros | tel. 928 56 06 09 | topdiving.net)*, in Puerto Rico; they also have their own decompression chamber. The *Cordial Mogán Playa* hotel in Puerto de Mogán has the *Delphinus Diving School (Av. de los Marreros 2 | tel. 607 05 47 15 | delphinus.eu/diving-gran-canaria)*, that provides an excellent diving base. In the north of the island, *Buceo Norte (Sardina del Norte | tel. 928 88 38 07 | buceonorte.com)* organizes diving excursions in the bay of Sardina.

GOLF

There are several year-round 18-hole courses. All have a driving range, club house, golf school and shop. Spain's oldest course (1891), the *Real Club de Golf de Las Palmas (realclubgolfdelaspalmas.com)*, has a delightful location high in the mountains near Santa Brígida. You need to book in advance.

There are several charming golf courses in the south: *Campo de Golf Maspalomas (maspalomasgolf.net)*, *Meloneras Golf (lopesan.com)*, *Salobre Golf (salobregolfresort.com)*

Meeting with a ray-like angel shark on the seafloor

and *Anfi Tauro Golf (anfi.com)* in the Valle de Tauro between Puerto Rico and Puerto de Mogán.

HIKING
For centuries, only the *caminos reales* (paths that were under the direct control of the crown) connected isolated villages with each other. After the introduction of tarmac roads, these *caminos* fell into oblivion. However, people started to repair them again as tourism developed and now many have been surfaced and signposted. But don't ever set out on the spur of the moment as it is easy to get lost in the mountainous terrain. A good guidebook is essential (available, for example at *Las Palmas Bike Station*, see p 51).

If you prefer to hike in a group, there are many organised tours to choose from. *Canco Gran Canaria*, for example, offers tours along the coast and in the mountains *(tel. 928 17 83 29 | cancograncanaria.com)*.

MINIGOLF
You can play minigolf in the holiday resorts such as Playa del Inglés in the *Centro Comercial Yumbo (Av. de Estados Unidos)*, at the *Hotel Atlántico (Av. de Tenerife 1)* and the *Hotel Maritim Playa (Av. de Tenerife 13 | all at: minigolfgrancanaria.com)*. However, the most beautiful minigolf course is at Playa de Amadores where you play in a maritime-style landscape, surrounded by mermaids, giant mussels and sharks *(Minigolf Neptuno | Av. Tomás Roca Bosch 4)*.

SAILING
Sailors can charter yachts in Puerto de Mogán, which is also home to the

(English-speaking) sailing school *Aistrac (trial, beginner and advanced courses from 240 euros | C/ Juan Deniz 10 | tel. 928 56 59 31 | aistrac.com)*.

SKYDIVING

You can glide like a bird with the well-established operator *SkyDive (tandem jump approx. 250 euros | tel. 675 57 32 45 | skydivegrancanaria.es)*. At the San Agustín airfield, a small aircraft will take you up to a height of 3,000 or 4,000m, and then you – and your experienced partner – will jump, to land in the dunes a few minutes later. Parachute courses are also offered.

SURFING, SUP & WINDSURFING

The reliable northeast trade winds mean that windsurfing is very popular. Beginners will find it easier in the south in winter (wind force 3–6), especially in sheltered bays such as Puerto Rico. Expert windsurfers will relish the superb conditions in the north in summer (wind force 5–9), with the best location being Pozo Izquierdo (always 6+).

Good spots for surfing are on the north coast. The best are at the southern and northern ends of Playa de las Canteras beach in Las Palmas (*Cícer* and *El Confital*). World Cup qualifying contests are held there every year. Whether you're a beginner or a pro, surf camps offer all kinds of courses and programmes, some including accommodation and excursions (see p. 51, e.g. *Mojo Surf | mojosurf.es*).

Wherever the surf isn't too strong, you can try stand-up paddle boarding, for example in Las Palmas, Playa de la Verga, Puerto Rico/Playa Amadores and Puerto de Mogán.

Surfing at Las Canteras

REGIONAL OVERVIEW

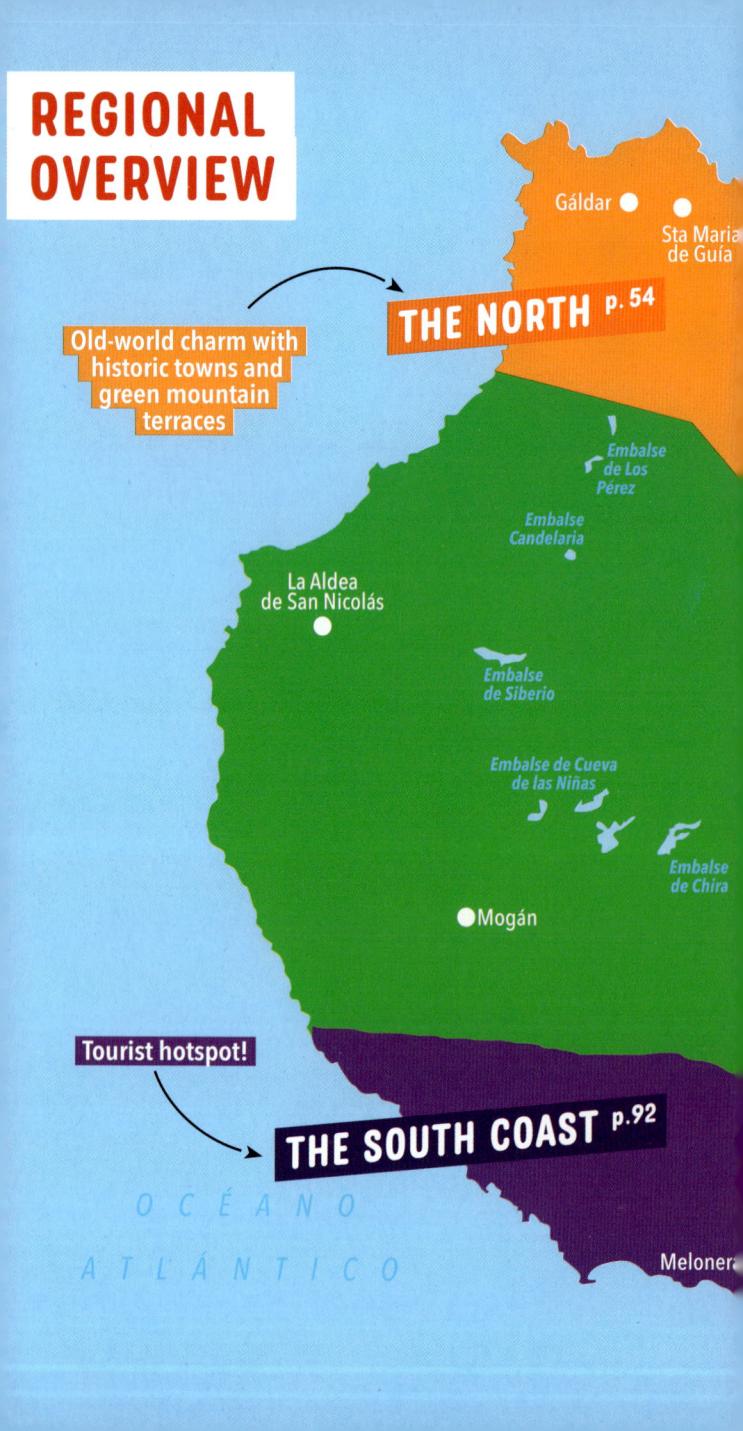

Old-world charm with historic towns and green mountain terraces

THE NORTH p. 54

- Gáldar
- Sta Maria de Guía
- Embalse de Los Pérez
- Embalse Candelaria
- La Aldea de San Nicolás
- Embalse de Siberio
- Embalse de Cueva de las Niñas
- Embalse de Chira
- Mogán

Tourist hotspot!

THE SOUTH COAST p. 92

OCÉANO ATLÁNTICO

Melonera

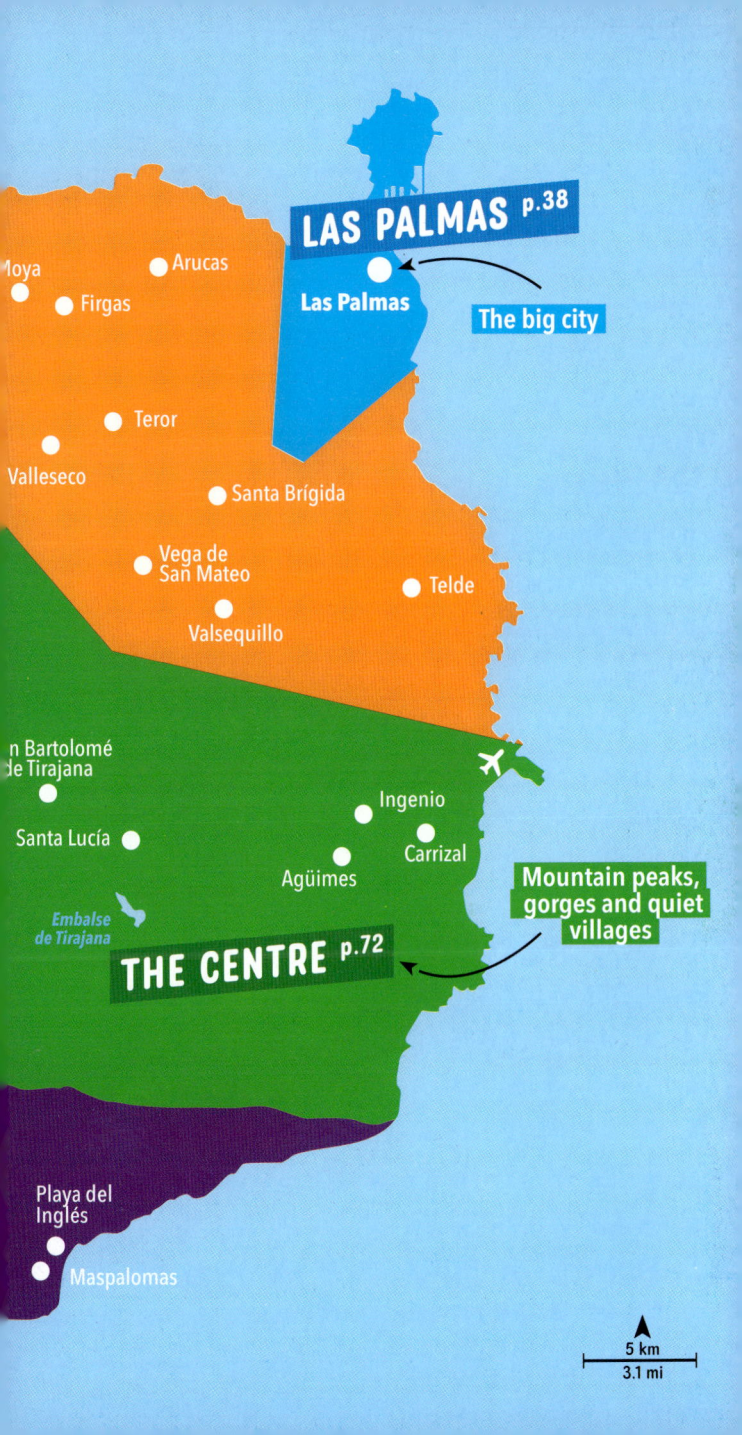

LAS PALMAS p.38

Las Palmas — The big city

Moya
Firgas
Arucas
Valleseco
Teror
Santa Brígida
Vega de San Mateo
Valsequillo
Telde

San Bartolomé de Tirajana
Santa Lucía
Agüimes
Ingenio
Carrizal

Embalse de Tirajana

THE CENTRE p.72

Mountain peaks, gorges and quiet villages

Playa del Inglés
Maspalomas

5 km
3.1 mi

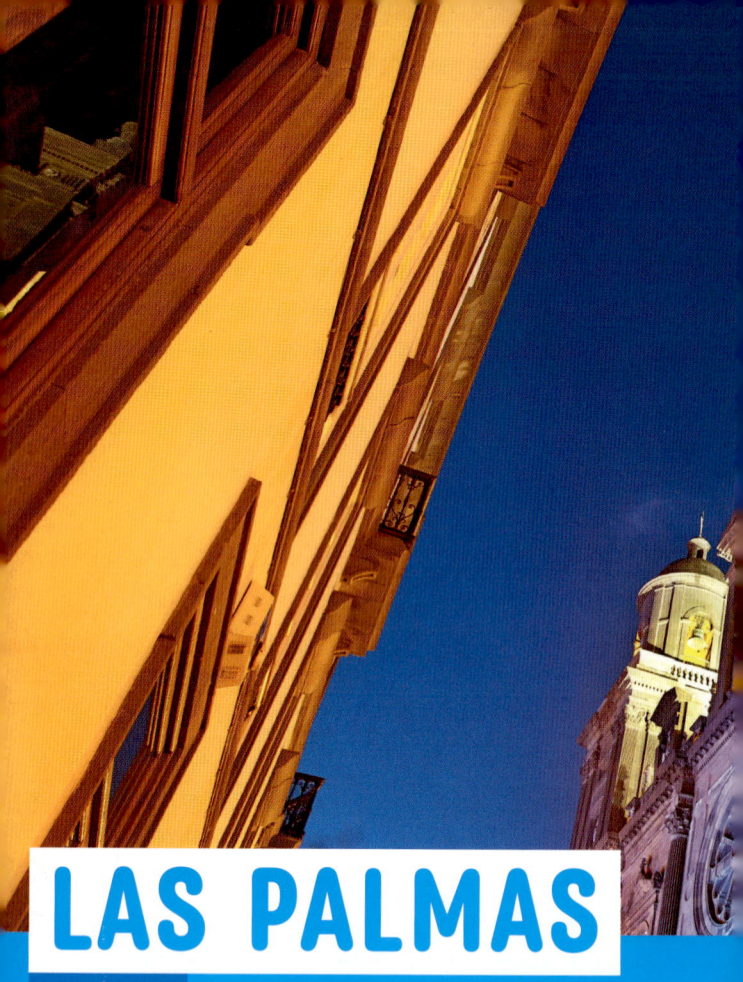

LAS PALMAS
ACTION!

Coming from the airport, you will pass sprawling tower-block neighbourhoods which stretch high into the mountains. This is where many of Las Palmas' 385,000 inhabitants live. But don't be put off by this first, negative impression, because the view improves once you get to the *La Vegueta* quarter.

It was here, where a gorge meets the sea, that Las Palmas was founded in 1483 as Spain's first ever colonial town. At its heart is a big plaza with a cathedral, town hall and palaces, surrounded by

The cathedral of Santa Ana towers above the old town of Las Palmas

grand streets. Subsequently, the design of Las Palmas was exported to all other Spanish colonies.

Gran Canaria's capital has far more to offer than beautiful architecture. The sea, of course, is ever-present, and the people, the Canarios, know about the art of living. At festivals they celebrate art and music, and anything and everything that creates joy. And that is highly infectious! Vegueta, the old town of Las Palmas, has a majestic beauty but also a somewhat sleepy atmosphere.

LAS PALMAS

- El Padrino
- La Oliva
- 100 Montaditos
- Mercado del Puerto 16
- **Acuario Poema del Mar** ★ 15
- El Tendedero de Catalina
- Museo Elder 14
- Parque de Santa Catalina 13
- Rastro
- Chester Club & Lounge
- Bululú Canarias
- Marrakech
- Granier
- El Corte Inglés
- **Playa de las Canteras** ★
- Bimba y Lola
- Museo Néstor
- Pueblo Canario and Parque Doramas 11 12
- **Jardín Canario** ★
- Catedr

MARCO POLO HIGHLIGHTS

★ **CATHEDRAL & PLAZA DE SANTA ANA**
The capital's royal core ➤ p. 42

★ **CASA DE COLÓN**
A magnificent palace with romantic patios ➤ p. 43

★ **CAAM (CENTRO ATLÁNTICO DE ARTE MODERNO)**
Contemporary art in a historic palace ➤ p. 43

★ **MUSEO CANARIO**
Learn all about the island's indigenous population ➤ p. 44

★ **ACUARIO POEMA DEL MAR**
Europe's biggest aquarium takes you deep down under the sea ➤ p. 46

★ **PLAYA DE LAS CANTERAS**
Lively and busy 4km-long beach and promenade ➤ p. 51

★ **JARDÍN CANARIO**
All kinds of exotic Canarian plants in an extensive botanical garden ➤ p. 53

Neighbouring Triana is quite a contrast! This is the merchants' quarter where people come to shop and browse for hours in the ever-expanding pedestrian zones. Next to the Triana is the Ciudad Jardín, the "garden city", an oasis for the wealthy Canarios. To the north, at the beginning of La Isleta peninsula, is El Puerto, the hub between Europe, Africa and America. This quarter was created in the 1960s, at the onset of tourism, and its 4km-long Canteras Beach and promenade is one of the top attractions of Las Palmas.

SIGHTSEEING

For 20 euros, you can spend a whole day on the *guagua turística* (tourist bus), travelling between the sights and getting on and off whenever and wherever you like. The red double-deckers leave from the Parque Santa Catalina in the harbour and beach quarter *(daily 9.30am–5.45pm, every 30 mins | city-sightseeing.com).*

WHERE TO START?

Plaza de Santa Ana: Take the bus to **Vegueta**, the Old Town. The express buses 30/50 connect the south with Las Palmas. If you're driving, park near the Mercado de la Vegueta. And if you want to visit the beach, use the multi-storey car parks in the shopping centres of **Las Arenas/El Muelle**. Taxis within the city cost 5–6 euros.

1 CATHEDRAL & PLAZA DE SANTA ANA ★

Plaza de Santa Ana is the main square of Vegueta, the Old Town of Las Palmas. The colonial-period *Catedral de Santa Ana* and town hall are situated on the vast square. At the end is the *Casa Consistorial* (old town hall with tourist information centre), while opposite, the Canarians' most magnificent church soars up into the heavens. Construction of the vast, five-aisled cathedral began in 1497, and it wasn't completed until the 19th century! Its long history is reflected in the architecture: the columns are Gothic, the façade neoclassical, the high altar baroque, and yet the overall effect is one of balanced coherence. The vault is particularly appealing for the piers that were made to resemble palm trees – a reference to the name "Las Palmas".

Please bear in mind that photography and speaking loudly are taboo during 🐷 mass (which is free to attend). Take the lift up the church tower and enjoy the views over the roofs of the Old Town!

Another lovely sight is the green "courtyard of the oranges" *(Patio de los Naranjos)* in the *Museo Diocesano de Arte Sacro*. The architecture is spectacular, as are the paintings, silver goblets and relics on display. *Visits to the cathedral outside services are possible through the Museo Diocesano de Arte Sacro. Tower Mon–Fri 10am–4.30pm, Sat 10am–1.30pm, services Mon–Fri 8–10am, Sat/Sun 8–9.30am and 6–8pm | combined museum and cathedral ticket 3 euros, tower additional 1.50 euros |* ⏱ *30 mins*

LAS PALMAS

Model ships bring historic seafaring to life

2 CASA DE COLÓN ⭐

"Columbus House" is a fabulous colonial building, delightful both on the outside and the inside. This is where the Spanish Governors used to reside. Now the museum highlights the connections between Gran Canaria and the New World because, after all, Columbus set sail to America from here in 1492. The Museum Shop sells original souvenirs, inspired by local folklore, such as *Mirita* brand T-shirts by designer Miriam Godoy. *Plaza Pilar Nuevo s/n | Mon-Fri 10am-6pm, Sat/Sun 10am-3pm | admission 4 euros | C/ Colón 1 | casadecolon.com | ⏱ 1 hr*

INSIDER TIP
The Canaries brand

3 ERMITA DE SAN ANTONIO ABAD

This is where Columbus prayed before setting off in 1492 to cross the endless expanse of the Atlantic Ocean. Well, that's according to the plaque on the façade of the chapel, which was built shortly before the historic date, making it the oldest church on the island. *Plaza de San Antonio Abad*

4 CAAM (CENTRO ATLÁNTICO DE ARTE MODERNO) ⭐

The *CAAM* displays temporary exhibitions of modern art in light and airy rooms. It is hidden behind the façades of the old houses on the best-preserved street in Vegueta, the Calle Los Balcones, behind Catedral Santa Ana *(Tue-Sat 10am-9pm, Sun 10am-2pm | admission free | C/ Los*

43

Balcones 9–11 | caam.net | 30 mins). Just a few minutes' walk away is a second site in the former hospital of *San Martín (C/ Ramón y Cajal 1/ corner of Sor Jesús)*. With its painstakingly restored inner courtyards and halls, the 18th-century neoclassical building offers a high-contrast framework for contemporary art. Also take a look into the small chapel.

Gáldar, as well as scenes of everyday life. In addition, there are skulls, skeletons and several well-preserved mummies in glass coffins. *Mon–Fri 10am–8pm, Sat/Sun 10am–2pm | admission 5 euros, children under 12 free | C/ Doctor Verneau 2 | elmuseocanario.com | 1hr*

If you feel the need for some greenery in Las Palmas, take a break in the Parque Doramas

5 MUSEO CANARIO ★

Learn about the Guanches, the indigenous people of Gran Canaria: the museum houses the biggest collection of ancient Canarian finds in the archipelago, including the *Idol of Tara*, a clay female figure that probably symbolises fertility. There is also a replica of the *Cueva Pintada* from

6 GABINETE LITERARIO

This lovely 19th-century Art Nouveau palace is on one of the most beautiful squares in town. Take a look inside where galleries several storeys high surround an atrium. Concerts are often held in the "Golden Salon", and there are also regular exhibitions. If you would like to enjoy a good meal

LAS PALMAS

and the views of the square, then go to *La Terraza del Gabinete* (see p. 48). *Plaza de Cairasco 1 | gabineteliterario.com*

7 CASA MUSEO PÉREZ GALDÓS

If you want to see how wealthy Canarians used to live, then visit the birthplace of one of Spain's leading literary figures. Many of Benito Pérez Galdós's (1843-1920) works, including *Halma*, *Tristana* and *Nazarín*, became world classics when they were made into films by Luis Buñuel. The house where he was born contains antique furniture and antiquarian prints, and you can find out more about contemporary literature in the smart modern extension. *Tue-Sun 10.30am-6.30pm, closed Sat/Sun in summer | admission 3 euros, children under 18 free | C/ Cano 2-6 | casamuseoperezgaldos.com | ⓘ 20 mins*

8 TEATRO PÉREZ GALDÓS

This fabulous theatre opposite the Old Town market was built in 1919 and is a combination of colonial style and Art Nouveau. The cubist extension complements it perfectly. Inside you can admire a "sky" of eroticising frescoes created by *Néstor de la Torre* (see p. 46). On the new plaza outside is a monumental sculpture of the writer Benito Pérez Galdós (1843-1920). *Plaza Stagno 1 | teatroperezgaldos.es*

9 PARQUE SAN TELMO

Remember this name if you're travelling by bus, because Las Palmas' main bus depot is underground. Above the ground – on the other side of a very busy road – is the actual park with palms and dragon trees as well as several pleasant pavilions. One of them contains the tourist office, and a second one, the *Kiosko San Telmo (irregular opening times)*, a pretty café with wood panelling.

10 CASA ÁFRICA

Africa House, an impressive 19th-century colonial building, contains works by artists from the "big neighbour", with pictures, films and music. It is located halfway between the Old Town and Ciudad Jardín. *Mon-Fri 9am-6pm | admission free | C/ Alfonso XIII 5 | casafrica.es | ⓘ 20 mins*

11 PUEBLO CANARIO & PARQUE DORAMAS

Pueblo Canario, the "Canarian Village", is situated halfway between the Old Town and the beach district. It was built in the pioneering days of the island's tourist industry (1939) in order to give visitors the impression of an intact rural idyll. What you see is a picturesque plaza surrounded by whitewashed buildings with balconies. One of them is the *Museo Néstor* (see p. 46). On Sundays at 11.30am there are performances of Canarian folklore song and dance.

Next door is the *Santa Catalina* 5-star hotel, built in the colonial style in 1980. From the hotel, head towards the yacht harbour, and you'll pass the statue of the last old Canarian ruler, Doramas, as he leapt to his death. *Parque Doramas* behind the hotel, an oasis of fountains and lush vegetation, is named after him.

12 MUSEO NÉSTOR

This little museum which was renovated in 2019 is a haven of peace and art in the *Pueblo Canario* in Ciudad Jardín. On display are paintings by the artist *Néstor Martín Fernando de la Torre* (1887–1938) that were inspired by the Canarian countryside and way of life, as well as his designs for houses, furniture and stage settings. *Tue–Sat 10am–7pm, Sun 10.30am–2.30pm | admission 2 euros | Pueblo Canario, Parque Doramas | las palmasgc.es/mnestor | ⏱ 30 mins*

13 PARQUE DE SANTA CATALINA

Las Palmas' biggest square is a large, landscaped area linking the harbour and the beach. There's always plenty going on here: cruise passengers, sailors and tourists passing through while Canarians play cards and chess under an awning. You can watch all the activity from the terrace cafés. A pretty little building in the middle of the square is the tourist office and next to it is the *Casa Fataga* restaurant which was designed by Miguel Martín de la Torre, brother of Néstor (see above). 🐦 On Saturdays from 11am you can listen to and watch folk singers and dancers in action, and the cruise passengers aren't the only ones who enjoy it! The neighbouring installation, created from coloured tiles and depicting the flags of every country on the planet, is certainly unusual.

14 MUSEO ELDER 🌴 👫

For all those who love experimenting! Visit the museum's fantastic website to get an idea what awaits you: an enigmatic, interactive look at everyday life: over three storeys, the science and technology museum, housed in a former warehouse for shipping goods, tells you all about gravity and attraction, macro and micro matter, earth and space. ==You can even climb into an aircraft cockpit and simulate a final approach.== *Tue–Sun 10am–8pm | admission 6 euros, children 3 euros | Parque de Santa Catalina | museoelder.org | ⏱ 1 hr*

INSIDER TIP
A perfect landing!

15 ACUARIO POEMA DEL MAR ★ 🌴 👫

Are you fascinated by sharks, gigantic goliath groupers or piranhas that can pull apart in seconds any animal that has fallen into the water? Europe's biggest aquarium promotes itself as a "window to the biodiversity of the world's oceans", showing key underwater habitats from coral reefs to the deep sea. *Daily 9am–6pm | admission 25 euros, children under 11 17.50 euros (additional 10 euros for the bus transfer from Costa Canaria and Costa Mogán) | Muelle del Sanapú 22 | tel. 928 01 03 50 | poema-del-mar.com | ⏱ 2 hrs*

16 CASTILLO DE LA LUZ

A "fortress of light" for modern art! Thick exposed walls contrast with filigree, floating iron creations by top sculptor Martín Chirino, who was born in Las Palmas in 1925. Glass walkways cross abysses, while labyrinthine corridors are reminiscent of 1493, when the tiny castle was built as protection against pirates. It proved its worth in 1595, when its canons were set against the English fleet of Sir Francis Drake. *Mon–Sat 10am–7pm, Sun 10am–2pm | admission 4 euros | C/ Juan Rejón | fundacionmartinchirino.org | ⏱ 30–45 mins*

EATING & DRINKING

100 MONTADITOS
Fast-food Canarian style. "The Spanish are not interested in eating quickly, but in having a good time enjoying great company." The outlets have a rustic design, ingredients and recipes are provided by the main site and a mini baguette *(montadito)* is not more than one or two euros. In Las Palmas you can find a *100 Montaditos* at the northern end of the Canteras Promenade. *Daily from 9am | Paseo de las Canteras 5 | spain.100montaditos.com | €*

BULULÚ CANARIAS
In the hidden-away mini restaurant with an informal atmosphere, chef Kike prepares high-level fusion cuisine. How about foie gras in a pistachio crust? You are advised to book a table. *Wed–Sun 1–4.30pm, 8–11pm | C/ Venezuela 4/corner Olof Palme | tel. 828 66 10 79 | FB: bululucanarias | €€*

EL PADRINO
This establishment, which opened in Las Coloradas on the Isleta peninsula in 1974, is extremely popular with the Canarians. The glass pavilion is a hive of activity at weekends, and fish is trumps. *Open daily | C/ Jesús Nazareno 1 | tel. 928 46 20 94 | FB: Restaurant El Padrino | €€*

Get your wings (on the ground) in Museo Elder

GRANIER 🐷
They bake the bread on site and offer a wide variety of toppings at a great price. You can either eat outside on the promenade or take away. *Canteras 12 and 61 | pansgranier.com | €*

LA OLIVA
Señora Lola's "Olive" sits on the northern edge of the promenade protected from the wind. The uncomplicated Spanish-Canarian cuisine and the speedy service ensure brisk business. At lunchtime, you can enjoy a fish dish on the terrace, but at night you should head to the rustic Bodega for wine and Iberian ham. *Open daily | Las Canteras | C/ Prudencio Morales 17 | tel. 928 46 97 57 | laolivarestaurante.com | €–€€*

LA TERRAZA DEL GABINETE
It's wonderful to sit on the covered terrace of the *Gabinete Literario* and look down on the lovely square. You should try the Mediterranean cuisine – especially the tuna carpaccio. *Closed Sun evening | Plaza de Cairasco 1 | tel. 928 43 14 12 | FB: Gabinete Restaurante | €€*

MARRAKECH
Delicacies from Africa: next-door neighbour of the Canaries Chef Ahmed Jerrari creates classics of North African cuisine, served in style: from lamb couscous to pastries from their own shop. *Daily 1-5pm, 8pm-midnight | C/ Juan Manuel Durán 46 | tel. 828 66 27 84 and 665 31 61 27 | FB: Marrakech Restaurante Las Palmas | €€*

> **INSIDER TIP**
> Arabian Nights pastry

MONTESDEOCA
This restaurant is arguably the prettiest in the capital and it serves fabulous food to boot. Surrounded by lush greenery in the romantic courtyard of a colonial building in the Vegueta, chef and author Fabio Santana serves creative Canarian cuisine from local seasonal produce: it's a delight for the senses. Prepare to be surprised! *Mon-Sat 1-4pm, 8pm-midnight | C/ Montesdeoca 10 | tel. 828 91 73 94 | FB: FabioSantanaCasaMontesdeoca | €€€*

> **INSIDER TIP**
> Foodie idyll

17 ZOE FOOD
The trend may have taken a while to reach the island, but now vegan restaurants and organic shops are popping up like mushrooms. In the Old Town the veggie scene meets at *Zoe Food*, where they offer two-course menus with a drink of your choice every day: healthy and cheap! You can eat either on the terrace or inside with a retro ambience. *Mon-Fri from 9am, Sat from 10am, Sun from 11am | C/ Domingo J Navarro 35 | tel. 928 58 65 07 | FB: Zoe Food Las Palmas | €*

SHOPPING

BIMBA & LOLA
Seen on the catwalk yesterday, available from Bimba & Lola today: accessories, shoes and bags with buzz, all made from high-quality materials. *Mon-Fri 10am-1.30pm, 5-8pm, Sat 10am-1.30pm | CC Las Arenas | Catalina | bimbaylola.com*

LAS PALMAS

Fresh fish in the Old Town at the Mercado de la Vegueta

CORTE INGLÉS

This traditional department store is the shopping temple of the well-off. The building on the north side of the boulevard is particularly interesting. It sells fashion and cosmetics, and in the basement is the longest fish counter in the Canary Islands. The island's wines are available from the wine department, and there's also a department selling the best-known dairy products – including *queso de flor*! You are welcome to try before you buy; just say *"Podría probar un trocito?"*, "May I try a little?" *Mon–Sat 9.30am–9.30pm | Av. Mesa y López 18 | Catalina | elcorteingles.es*

FEDAC

A very special address: the finest Canarian arts and crafts from woven handbags and traditional ceramics to silver jewellery, lace and embroidered tablecloths, in a side street off Triana. Exquisite, traditional, new – and even recycled – goods. *Mon–Fri 9.30am–1.30pm and 4.30–8pm | C/ Domingo J Navarro 7 | Triana | fedac.org*

LA LIBRERÍA

This small bookshop is devoted exclusively to the Canaries. There are good hiking guides, maps and background literature in many languages. *Mon–Fri 9.30am–1.30pm and 4.30–8pm, Sat 9.30am–1.30pm | C/ Cano 24/ Travieso | Triana | libroscanarios.org*

MASAP

In this delightful manor house in the Old Town you'll find unusual antiques, charmingly presented by Arantxa and Francisco. For example, there are 100-year-old prints as well as advertising signs from the 1950s, and small objets d'art by contemporary Canarian artists. *Mon–Fri 10am–1.30pm, 5–8pm, Sat 10am–1.30pm | C/ Alcalde Francisco Hernández González/corner C/ Juan Doreste 18 | Vegueta | anticuarioycoleccionista.com*

MERCADO DE LA VEGUETA

The market is the beating heart of the Old Town. The stalls are tightly packed next to each other in the huge hall; shoppers and visitors jostle their way past them. There are fruit and vegetables as well as a large selection of meat, fish, cheese and sausages. *Mon–Sat 8am–2pm | C/ Mendizábal 1 | FB: mercadovegueta*

MERCADO DEL PUERTO

It's a little quieter in the old market hall in the harbour, an iron construction in the style of Eiffel. There are some pleasant tapas and terrace bars, and the choice ranges from pinchos to pasta, sushi to Scandinavian. Great atmosphere on Friday and Saturday nights. *Market Mon–Sat 8am–2pm, bars Tue–Sat until midnight | C/ Albareda 76 | mercadodelpuerto.net*

INSIDER TIP — Weekend hotspot

In Las Palmas the beach is never far away: Playa de las Canteras

RASTRO 🐗

The Sunday flea market near Parque Santa Catalina attracts thousands of visitors every weekend. You can buy wooden African masks, Spanish fashion made in China, kitsch and commerce. There are also a few snack bars and live music, that makes rummaging around all the more fun!

SPORT & ACTIVITIES

CYCLING/HIKING

You can hire reasonably priced high-quality bicycles near Parque de Santa Catalina, plus exciting tours with the Hike & Bike shuttle service at *Las Palmas Bike Station (C/ 29 de Abril 63 | tel. 928 93 54 11, mobile tel. 605 06 10 24 | rental-bike-station-gran-canaria.com)*. They also sell up-to-date hiking guides.

SURFING

In those areas where the reef has a gap in Las Palmas, big Atlantic waves break on the coastline. Surfers love these conditions and enjoy the wild swell. Courses for all levels, with equipment and competent instructors, plus accommodation on request, are offered by *Oceanside Gran Canaria Surf (C/ Almansa 14 | tel. 928 22 04 37 | oceansidesurf.es)*.

Similar services are available from *Mojo Surf (Calle Perú 20/Playa de las Canteras | mojosurf.es | tel. 659 22 55 00)*.

BEACHES

Almost 4km of powdery sand cover several large bays below a wide beach promenade that ends in a wide arch. A reef protects the ⭐ 🌴 *Playa de las Canteras* against the strong surf. The waves are only suitable for surfing at the southern end, where there are gaps in the reef. The fortress-like concert house *Auditorio Alfredo Kraus* dominates the scene with the pyramid roofs of the *Las Arenas* shopping centre behind it. Las Canteras is often compared to the beaches of Rio de Janeiro and it actually has a lot of the Brazilian city's vivacity. There are public showers (free) and WCs.

NIGHTLIFE

Las Palmas lays on an excellent selection of cultural events, from a music and opera festival in winter to summer street theatre and jazz in the early autumn. It's busiest on Thursdays, Fridays and Saturdays. There are multiplex cinemas that show the latest films at the *Las Arenas (southern end Canteras Promenade)* and *El Muelle (Muelle de Santa Catalina)* shopping centres. A great spot to chill is between the Plaza de Cairasco and Triana on *Boulevard Monopol*, a small shopping centre with pubs, sandwich shops and cocktail bars. The most popular venue is *La Bohème (daily 10.30am–midnight, Fri/Sat until 2am)*, which has a large terrace and plays gentle pop music. Next door at the *Paper Club (Thu–Sat from 10pm | C/ Remedios 10)*, there's live music ranging from jazz to rock in an old, lovingly restored mansion house. Across the road, in the *Vegueta* quarter, a lively pub scene has developed in the pedestrian zone *(C/ Pelota/Mendizábal)*. The excellent-value 🐷 tapas night starts around 8.30pm on Thursdays. In the beach zone, people meet between the *Calle Franchy Roca* and the *Plaza de la Música*. The best atmosphere is on the *Plaza de Fray Junípero* where local musicians can often be heard. In the summer months, the *Canteras Promenade* is full of people late into the night. Music pubs such as *Tiramisú (Plaza del Pilar)* are extremely popular.

Las Palmas club scene: tapas, beer and dancing until the early hours

LAS PALMAS

CHESTER CLUB & LOUNGE
A popular mainstream meeting place at weekends, only a few steps from the Parque de Santa Catalina. They play pop, salsa and Latin on the – admittedly – small dance floor. The atmosphere is relaxed, there is no dress code and the minimum age is 25. While there is not much going on before midnight, the party lasts until dawn. *Fri/Sat 6pm-6am | C/ Simón Bolívar 3*

EL TENDEDERO DE CATALINA
It's fun and funky on the roof of the *Bed & Chic* hotel. A DJ spins the decks, and the perfectly mixed cocktails and views of the harbour and illuminated cruise ships are fabulous. *Thu-Sun from 5.30pm | C/ General Vives 78 | Parque de Santa Catalina | FB: El Tendedero de Catalina*

INSIDER TIP — Below you the glittering sea

> ### WHERE TO STAY IN LAS PALMAS
>
> **IN THE THICK OF THINGS**
> If you want to stay where there is plenty of action, then the *BEX (98 rooms | C/ León y Castillo 330 | tel. 928 97 10 71 | designplusbexhotel.com | €€)* is the place for you. Located close to Parque de Santa Catalina, only a three-minute walk from the bus terminal and the beach, you can expect an eccentric interior: the hotel, a converted Art Deco building that was once the national bank, is decorated along the lines of money, with breakfast being served in the one-time bank safe!

AROUND LAS PALMAS

18 JARDÍN CANARIO ★ ⚑
10km / 10 mins southwest of Las Palmas via the GC 12/110
Just outside the villa suburb of Tafira Alta, in a pretty location on a slope in the valley of the Barranco de Guiniguada, is the "Canarian Garden". The park is a haven of peace. The plants, such as dragon tree, bay and euphorbia, are almost all Canarian. The garden with prickly exotics is impressive and includes cactus-like plants that are as wide as a tree trunk. There are also various small ponds with birds, an exhibition hall and a souvenir pavilion. Located at the upper entrance, the *Jardín Canario* restaurant (*Sun-Thu 10am-6pm, Fri-Sat 10am-midnight | Ctra del Centro | Tafira Baja | tel. 928 35 52 45 | restaurantejardincanario.com | €€*), serves excellent Canarian cuisine and has a nice view into the valley. *Daily 10am-6pm | admission free | entrance: right at Km1.7 (stairs!) on the GC 110 between Las Palmas and Tafira Alta; alternative, more convenient entrance on the GC 310 between Tamaraceite and Tafira Alta | ⏱ 1-2 hrs | 🗺 G3*

THE NORTH

WILD SURF & GREEN TERRACED FIELDS

The North is an antidote to the hyperactive capital. Here, life is quieter and more traditional. If you are coming from the South, the contrast is tremendous, and you'll be tempted to ask if you're still on the same island.

While the sun parches the earth in the South, here cooling trade winds brush the laurel and pine forests. They blow in towards the *cumbre* where they get caught and go no further. As a result, the ground never completely dries out and vegetation flourishes. The

Terraced fields near Vega de San Mateo

mild climate is perfect for farming. There are terraced fields wherever you look: avocados, citrus fruit, medlars, guavas and bananas. The North has beautiful historic towns, especially Teror, home to the Virgin of the Pine, and Arucas with its opulent church. However, you will also see some urban sprawl. Settlements have spread out wherever there is space. Apart from Playa de Melenara and Sardina, there are hardly any beaches. The ocean batters the rocky coastline and the white surf surges all down the coast.

THE NORTH

68km, 1½ hrs Santa Cruz (Tenerife)

9 Sardina del Norte

Museo y Parque Arqueológico Cueva Pintada ★

Gáldar p.68

Santa María de Guía p.66

8 Cenobio de Valerón ★

Moya und Parque Natural Los Tilos **6**

Moya

Firgas **5**

Puerto de las Nieves p.70

10 Agaete

11 Valle de Agaete

San Pedro

33km, 50 mins

7 Fontanales

Valleseco

Teror ★ p.62

43km, 1¼ hrs

Cruz de Tejeda

Tejeda

San Bartolomé de Tirajana

MARCO POLO HIGHLIGHTS

★ **CALDERA DE BANDAMA**
Gran Canaria's biggest crater at the foot of a cone-shaped mountain is a mere 1,800 years old! ➤ p.60

★ **TEROR**
Place of pilgrimage to honour the Virgin of the Pine ➤ p.62

★ **ARUCAS**
Home of the water barons, their mansions and gardens ➤ p.64

★ **CENOBIO DE VALERÓN**
Spectacular group of caves with 298 chambers covering an entire rock face ➤ p.67

★ **MUSEO Y PARQUE ARQUEOLÓGICO CUEVA PINTADA**
The "painted cave" is the most important legacy of the original inhabitants of the Canary Islands ➤ p.69

OCÉANO ATLÁNTICO

Las Palmas de Gran Canaria

Arucas ★ p. 64

15km, 15 mins

Tafira Baja

Pico de Bandama
4 **Caldera de Bandama** ★

● **Santa Brígida** p. 60

● **Vega de San Mateo** p. 61

3 Valsequillo

● **Telde** p. 58

2 Playa de Melenara

1 Cuatro Puertas

○ Urbanización Ojos de Garza

○ Ingenio

2 km
1.24 mi

TELDE

(□ H4) Telde, the second largest town on Gran Canaria (pop. almost 100,000), has atmospheric historic quarters that are worth visiting.

Coming from the motorway, keep right at the second roundabout in Telde for the *San Juan* district. The prettiest streets of the Old Town surround the *Basílica de San Juan Bautista*.

WHERE TO START?

Plaza de San Juan: It's easy to explore the historical San Francisco and San Juan districts starting from the square in front of the church. But, as it's difficult to find a place to park in one of the side streets, consider leaving your car on the western edge of the town and walking the 10–15 minutes to the historical centre.

SIGHTSEEING

PLAZA & BASÍLICA DE SAN JUAN BAUTISTA

The square in the centre of the San Juan quarter is an excellent example of colonial architecture. And the jewel in the crown is St John the Baptist church, Telde's most important church, which has a Gothic façade from 1520, flanked by bell towers in dark basalt cubes. The beautiful carved main altar is from Flanders, while the figure of Christ made out of maize pulp is from Mexico. *Usually only open during the services*

SAN FRANCISCO

A stroll through the dreamy San Francisco district is like a journey through ancient times. Low, whitewashed houses and tiny squares lie hidden along the narrow cobbled streets opposite Plaza San Juan. To reach them, turn right off *Calle Juan Carlos* through a narrow archway. In the centre is sunny *Plaza San Francisco* with the church of the same name. There is a wonderful view of the fertile *Barranco de San Miguel* from the balustrade.

> **INSIDER TIP**
> Here the clocks tick slowly!

THE NORTH

CASA MUSEO LEÓN Y CASTILLO
The old mansion with the faithfully reproduced interior is the birthplace of the brothers León y Castillo. Fernando was Spain's foreign secretary from 1881 and his brother Juan worked as an engineer and designed the modern port of Las Palmas. *Tue–Sun 10am–6pm | admission 2 euros | C/ León y Castillo 43*

EATING & DRINKING

VINOTECA SAN JUAN
Diagonally opposite the church you get a glass of good wine, accompanied by hearty tapas. *Closed Mon | Plaza de San Juan | €€*

AROUND TELDE

1 CUATRO PUERTAS
5km / 5 mins south of Telde via the GC 100

The "Mountain of Four Gates" – once a sacred site of the indigenous Canarians – looks like a giant skull with wide open eyes. It has four massive rectangular entrances as well as sacrificial altars and a congregating area. *Admission free | on the GC 100 after Ingenio | ⏲ 1 hr | 🗺 H4*

The charming town of Telde with its colonial-style houses

SANTA BRÍGIDA

2 PLAYA DE MELENARA
7km / 14 mins southwest of Telde via the GC 10 and GC 116
This 400-m-long beach of dark sand is in a small bay protected from the currents by rocks. It is packed with local families at weekends. There is a wide promenade, a playground for children and green spaces. | *H4*

3 VALSEQUILLO
11km / 15 mins west of Telde via the GC 41
It is easy to see how important agriculture is here: the town is surrounded by some of the loveliest groves of almond trees on the island and the valley is transformed into a sea of white blossom in February. From May, the branches are laden with light-brown almonds. The road is also lined with fig trees. *Sidra* (cider) and fruit vinegar are made from the apples. The lush greenery feeds cows, sheep and goats whose milk is used to make delicious cheeses. *F–G4*

SANTA BRÍGIDA

(*F-G3*) **This is where tourism on Gran Canaria began in the 19th century. Wealthy Brits spent the winter in the fresh mountain air and played golf on Spain's first ever golf course. With its shady avenues, subtropical gardens and pretty villas, Santa Brígida has remained a place of affluence even if tourism has long shifted towards the coast.**

The historic Old Town centre is nicely restored and has a church square with plenty of good views. At the spruced-up *Casa del Vino (closed Sat | GC 15, Km3.9)* on the main road through town, you can taste some of the island's wines. Below this "house of wine", you'll find the municipal park with its vegetable gardens, fruit trees, palm groves and petting zoo *(admission free)*.

EATING & DRINKING

MARTELL
Exquisite meat dishes go well with a glass of red house wine. After a great meal in this rustic restaurant you may find it hard to go home. *Daily noon–5pm, 8pm–midnight (closed Sept) |GC 15, Km8.3 (El Madroñal) | tel. 928 64 12 83 | €€*

AROUND SANTA BRÍGIDA

4 CALDERA DE BANDAMA/PICO DE BANDAMA
10km / 15 mins east of Santa Brígida via the GC 110/800
The panoramic view over the northeast of the island and Las Palmas from the *Pico de Bandama* (574m) is quite stunning. It borders the ★ *Caldera de Bandama*, the crater of an extinct

THE NORTH

A hiking trail leads from Bandama right into the caldera

volcano which, with a diameter of 1,000m, is the largest on Gran Canaria. You can hike over the crumbly lava stones to a small farm 200m down at the bottom. It'll take you an hour *(but remember that the entrance at the top closes around 5pm!)*.

Right next to the crater, you will find Spain's oldest golf course (1891) nestled among the volcanic hills. You can enjoy this fantastic landscape with cones, craters and rolling greens around the clock at *Bandama Golf Hotel*. It is surrounded by Gran Canaria's oldest vineyards, where grapes ripen on mineral-rich lava substrate. You can buy the wine in the *Bodega Hoyos de Bandama (Camino a la Caldera 36)* next to the crater entry. Also fun is a visit to the atmospheric *Bodegón Vandama (closed Mon/Tue | GC 802, Km2.4 | tel. 928 35 27 54 | bodegonvandama.com | €€)* close by, which is a family-run winery at the foot of the volcano. Earthy organic wine and tender meat go well together. You grill the latter on a table-top griddle *(brasero)* to suit your taste. The views from the terrace stretch across slopes of vines to the volcano, and inside you can sit in front of the old grape press. | *G3*

INSIDER TIP Earthy food and wine

VEGA DE SAN MATEO

(*F3–4*) **The mountain village (pop. 8,000) at an altitude of 850m is much more peaceful and interesting than the wide main street and**

Where to begin? Sunday market in Teror

TEROR

(*III F3*) **If there was a contest for the "most Canarian" place of all, the town of ★ ⚑ Teror (pop. 12,000), at an altitude of 540m in the northern *cumbre* region, would definitely win it.**

Everything about Teror – its architecture, religious importance and culinary delights – has a special quality. The village seems to huddle around the massive basilica. In front of it, tranquil *Plaza del Pino* is shaded by an ancient pine tree and surrounded by dazzling white townhouses with bleached wooden balconies and red roof tiles. On top of this, there are the well-preserved façades of the houses on *Calle Real de*

bus station would make you think at first.

Old townhouses along narrow, winding streets seem to be lost in their dreams. The town hall and church are located opposite each other on a small square. The locals live mainly from farming, and a famous cattle market attracts visitors from all over the island on Sundays. Then you can shop for food and crafts in San Mateo, as the locals call it for short.

EATING & DRINKING

ALPENDRE DE LA VEGA
Try their stew with forest cress or chickpeas, accompanied by a glass of local wine. *Fri/Sat 1–4pm and 8–11pm, Sun 1–5pm | C/ El Retiro 5 | GC 15, Km11.8 | tel. 928 66 12 79 | €*

la Plaza ("street of balconies"). The entire Old Town of Teror is listed.

After indigenous Canarian shepherds had reported that the Virgin Mary had appeared to them in a pine tree on 8 September 1481, the Pope declared the apparition a miracle and Teror rapidly developed into the most important place of pilgrimage in the entire archipelago. The festivities last an entire month, although the town is busiest on 8 September when thousands celebrate the festival of the Virgin of the Pine (Virgen del Pino).

Nevertheless, you can enjoy a wonderful day here at other times: slowly wander through the streets, admire the dragon tree on the small, fenced square opposite the basilica, buy a souvenir at the ceramics stand and have a cup of coffee in one of the bars.

SIGHTSEEING

BASÍLICA DE NUESTRA SEÑORA DEL PINO

Even non-churchgoers like to look inside this place of worship. The baroque building was completed in 1767 in the exact spot where the pine tree grew and where 15th-century shepherds had an apparition of the Virgin Mary. All that remained of the old church after an explosion was the tower, which was incorporated in the new building.

Inside the basilica are several baroque, lavishly gold-plated main and side altars. A cross relic of the wood of the legendary pine tree is stored under glass, and still venerated by devout souls.

Behind the church is the entrance to the *Museo Diocesano de Arte Sacro* with the Virgin's treasures – all of them donations! *Church Mon–Fri 9am–1pm and 3.30–7.45pm, Sat 9am–8pm, Sun 7.30am–7.30pm | admission free | museum Mon–Fri 1–3pm, Sat/Sun 10am–3pm | museum admission 1.50 euros | 30 mins*

EATING & DRINKING

CAFETERÍA LA PLAZA

This pleasant bar opposite the baroque basilica – popular with local people – is a good place to relax over a cup of tea and a biscuit after a visit to the church. *Open daily | Plaza del Pino 1 | €*

TASCA EL ENCUENTRO

This terrace restaurant on the church square serves small dishes, hams and local cheeses. *Closed Mon | Plaza del Pino 7 | tel. 928 63 26 07 | €*

SHOPPING

SUNDAY MARKET

On Sunday mornings, a large food, crafts and flea market is held around the basilica. You can also buy specialities from Teror such as spicy chorizo sausage, which tastes great on a fresh aniseed roll *(panecillo con matalauva)*. Best to get there early before the crowds and the traffic jams!

INSIDER TIP: Hot dog!

ARUCAS

Fake Gothic: Arucas' church was built in the 20th century

ARUCAS

(F2) **A historic centre with promenades for seeing and being seen, a fabulous church and a flourishing rum factory: there are signs everywhere indicating that ★ Arucas (pop. 34,000) is a prosperous town.**

The name of the rum *(arehucas)* comes from a settlement of the indigenous Canarians that was once located here. Enormous quantities of sugar cane were grown on the northern slopes of the *cumbre* as early as the 16th century, and distilleries were soon established. A large percentage of the laurel tree forests were felled so that the area could be cultivated. An upturn in the banana trade at the end of the 19th century, contributed to the wealth of the large landowners, and in 1900 they had the island's prettiest church built.

SIGHTSEEING

IGLESIA DE SAN JUAN BAUTISTA
The Church of St John the Baptist is as big as a cathedral. From a distance, it looks like a Gothic masterpiece, but it was actually built in the early 20th century. The large rosette window above the main portal, the pillars and the fan vaulting above are fabulous. *Usually open during the day*

THE NORTH

PARQUE MUNICIPAL
In this well-kept park, strelitzias and bougainvillea, hibiscus and other gloriously coloured exotic plants flourish in lavish profusion. They are irrigated by a sophisticated system of canals, reminding visitors of Arucas' abundant supply of water. On the edge of the park, works by Canarian artists are exhibited in the *Museo Municipal (Mon–Fri 10am–6pm, Sat 10am–1pm | admission free | Plaza de la Constitución 3)*.

MONTAÑA DE ARUCAS
The road spirals its way around the hill in the town, rising to a good 400m. When you reach the top, you will have a fine view in all directions, including a panorama of the dark-green banana plantations, some of which are covered with plastic sheeting. *1km*

AREHUCAS
The keen-eyed will recognise it by the tall chimney: inaugurated in 1884, the spirits produced at this distillery quickly gained recognition throughout the country. The guided tour includes the bodega where the rum barrels bear autographed messages of thanks from celebrity visitors. At the end of the tour you can enjoy a rum tasting. *Mon–Fri 9am–2pm, in summer until 1pm | admission 2.50 euros | Era de San Pedro 2 | arehucas.es | 1 hr*

JARDÍN DE LA MARQUESA
There is an abundance of fabulous exotic plants in this magical botanic garden a little outside the town. The "Garden of the Marchioness" is full of dragon trees and palms from all over the world, and proud peacocks strut their feathers by a pond. It's fun for the children too. *Mon–Fri 9am–1pm and 2–6pm, Sat 9am–1pm | admission 6 euros | jardindelamarquesa.com | GC 330 towards Bañaderos, 1km | 1 hr*

EATING & DRINKING

TASCA JAMÓN JAMÓN
On the main route to the church: they serve various categories of Iberian ham, cut wafer-thin. *C/ León y Castillo 5–6 | €*

AROUND ARUCAS

5 FIRGAS
8km / 10 mins southwest of Arucas via the GC 300

Order mineral water on Gran Canaria, and you'll usually be brought a bottle of the exellent *Firgas*, either lightly sparkling *(con gas)* or still *(sin gas)*. You can hear babbling fountains all over the town, and one flows in a cascade down a street. The centre around the *Plaza San Roque* with the pretty church is well worth visiting. On your way, you'll see a restored mill from 1512, and behind it the sculpture of a man with a cow – in honour of Firgas' industrious farmers. *E–F2*

SANTA MARÍA DE GUÍA

6 MOYA & PARQUE NATURAL LOS TILOS

13km / 15 mins west of Arucas via the GC 300/350

A large church, *Iglesia del Pilar*, towers over this sleepy little town (pop. 3,000) in the foothills of the *cumbre*. Diagonally opposite is the *birthplace of Tomás Morales (Mon–Fri 9am–8pm, Sat/Sun 10am–2pm | admission 2 euros | C/ del Poeta Tomás Morales | 30 mins)* (1884–1921), a doctor who is known all over Spain as a poet.

Two kilometres south of Moya, the GC 704 turns off to the *Los Tilos* nature reserve. At the dark bottom of the *Barranco del Laurel* you can see what remains of Gran Canaria's once-extensive laurel forests. The evergreen trees grow in close proximity to each other, protected from the sun's heat by the mountains. From the small *Centro de Interpretación* visitor centre *(admission free)* you can walk on a 2-km circular trail or follow the narrow lane through the gorge to Fontanales. 1 hr | E2

> **INSIDER TIP**
> Walk under laurel trees

7 FONTANALES

18km / 25 mins southwest of Arucas via the GC 75

This is a village between green hills. Because the two churches are usually closed, you can head straight for the restaurant: the *Sibora (open daily | C/ Juan Mateo de Castro 6 | tel. 928 62 04 24 | FB: Restaurante Grill Sibora | €€)* serves generous portions of hearty Canarian classics and is a popular destination for the locals. E3

SANTA MARÍA DE GUÍA

(D–E1) **Guía – locals never call this town (pop. 15,000) by its full name – is atmospheric with a quiet historical centre.**

Cuchillos canarios, the sharp Canarian knives known for their finely embellished handles, are a speciality of Guía. And then, of course, there's the best Canarian cheese. Both are for sale in the *Tienda de Arturo* (see p. 67).

SIGHTSEEING

IGLESIA DE LA ASUNCIÓN

The most interesting features in the interior of this 18th-century church are the statue of Christ on the main altar and several figures of the Virgin. These works are by Luján Pérez (1756–1815), the greatest Canarian sculptor. *Irregular opening hours | Plaza*

MUSEO NÉSTOR ÁLAMO

Canarian folk! A music museum in a historic house near the church square is dedicated to Néstor Álamo (1906–94) who made Canarian folklore known to the world. *Mon–Sat 10am–3pm | admission 1 euro | C/ San José 7 | museonestoralamo.com | 20 mins*

EATING, DRINKING & SHOPPING

TIENDA DE ARTURO

This ancient shop with adjoining bar

THE NORTH

sells cheese and ham tapas as well as the famous ⚑ "flower cheese" *(queso de flor, see p. 28)*, plus excellent red wine. In addition, you can buy baskets and other woven items and *cuchillos canarios* (Canarian knives) – they're not cheap, but they will last you a lifetime. *Daily 9am–7pm | tel. 928 88 08 08 | GC 292, at the edge of the village, direction Gáldar | €*

AROUND SANTA MARÍA DE GUÍA

8 CENOBIO DE VALERÓN ★
5km / 10 mins east of Guía via the GC 291

This impressive ensemble of caves was used by the indigenous people of Gran Canaria who painstakingly chiselled 298 niches and chambers out of the soft tuff stone. The caves seem to be stuck like swallows' nests in a kind of dome that is open to the north. For a long time, it was thought that these were the cells of a convent (Spanish: cenobio) for young women preparing to become high priestesses. However, it now seems certain that this labyrinth of caves was used at the time for storing grain. *Tue–Sun 10am–5pm | admission 3 euros, combined ticket with other archaeological sites 10 euros | GC 291, exit the GC 2 at Guía/Moya, to the left through the tunnel and then, at the roundabout, head towards Cuesta de Silva |* ⏱ *30 mins |* 📖 *E2*

Casa Tomás Morales in Moya is dedicated to the poet's life

GÁLDAR

(D1) **At the foot of the former volcanic cone of Pico de Gáldar lies Gáldar (pop. 23,000), capital of one of the two ancient Canarian kingdoms before the Spanish conquest.**

Take a stroll along the pedestrianised Calle Capitán Quesada to the *Plaza de Santiago*, one of the most picturesque squares in the Canaries, with the impressive pilgrimage church *Iglesia de Santiago*. The large square, shaded by conifers, is full of life all day long. The town has a long history, commemorated, above all, in the *Cueva Pintada*, the legendary "painted cave" in Gáldar's excavated settlement.

SIGHTSEEING

EL DRAGO

Gáldar boasts the oldest dragon tree on Gran Canaria. The magnificent specimen was planted in 1718 and its enormously thick trunk is now almost too wide for the arcaded patio of the *Casa Consistorial (visits usually only possible when the tourist office in the town hall is open on workdays until 1pm | Plaza de Santiago 1)*. Take a look next door into the *Teatro* with its sensational, painted vaulted ceiling. The Canarian artist Pepe Dámaso painted dragon trees that are intertwined with human bodies in a spiral.

INSIDER TIP: Look up!

Gáldar sits at the foot of the mountain of the same name

THE NORTH

IGLESIA DE SANTIAGO DE LOS CABALLEROS
Gáldar's 18th-century early Classical church with its twin towers rises up behind Plaza de Santiago. The sober interior contrasts with the valuable treasures that are displayed in the *Museo Sacro. Mon–Fri 5.30–7.30pm | admission 5 euros*

MUSEO ANTONIO PADRÓN 🌴
The paintings and sculptures by Antonio Padrón (1920–1968) take us back to an archaic world where the memory of the Guanches lives on. The museum is housed in the artist's former home/studio, which has been extensively refurbished. *Tue–Sat 10am–6pm | admission 2 euros | C/ Drago 2 | antoniopadron.com | ⏲ 30 mins*

MUSEO Y PARQUE ARQUEOLÓGICO CUEVA PINTADA ★ 🌴
In the archaeological park you'll find the entrance to the famous "painted cave", whose colourful geometric wall paintings are the most impressive testament to the island's first inhabitants. The cave is the main attraction of a partly excavated, partly reconstructed, settlement with dozens of circular buildings. You can go into some and get an idea of how the native Canarian population once lived. Background information in several languages is provided at the multimedia stations.

Excavated finds are exhibited in the museum: small idols, clay seals, jewellery and tools. You can buy arts and crafts inspired by old-Canarian artefacts in the museum shop (jewellery, ceramics, textiles and woven items). *Tue–Sat 10am–6pm, Sun 11am–6pm; admission until 4.30pm | admission 6 euros | C/ Audiencia 2 | cuevapintada.org | ⏲ 1.5 hrs*

EATING & DRINKING

CA' JUANCRI
Popular and typical bar in an old townhouse with high ceilings. A good place for tapas as well as delicious tortillas. *Open daily | C/ Tagoror 2–5 | near the town hall | €*

AROUND GÁLDAR

🟠 SARDINA DEL NORTE 🌴
6km / 6 mins northwest of Gáldar via the GC 202
This village, which has a pretty beach and a few fish restaurants, is on the outermost northern peak of the harsh coast. Enjoy sea views as you dine at *La Fragata (closed Wed | tel. 928 88 32 96 | €€€)*, a traditional establishment that serves fresh seafood and fish. The restaurant's interior – helm, portholes and lights – has been reclaimed from a decommissioned ship. You'll have the place almost to yourself during the week and will be able to plunge into the waves on the small, bright beach. 📖 *C1*

PUERTO DE LAS NIEVES

(C2) **The "snowy harbour" (pop. 1,000) is situated against a backdrop of dramatic cliffs which often turn a tremendous red colour at sunset. You will have an excellent view of this spectacle of nature from almost all the terraced restaurants in the evening.**

This fishing village owes its name to the "Virgin of the Snow" *(Virgen de las Nieves)* to whom the local chapel is dedicated. After you have visited the Madonna, go to the gravel-and-sand beach by the old pier, from where you can see the "Finger of God" *(Dedo de Dios)*, a rock needle which lost its tip in 2005 during tropical storm Delta. From the new pier, catamaran ferries operated by *Fred Olsen Express (fred olsen.es)* depart to Tenerife several times a day *(travelling time 1 hr | return ticket approx. 100 euros/pers).*

SIGHTSEEING

VIRGEN DE LAS NIEVES
The tiny chapel is home to some unusual model ships: votive offerings by fishermen who have been rescued at sea by the "Virgin of the Snow". *Usually open during the day*

EATING & DRINKING

DEDO DE DIOS
This restaurant on the old pier has panoramic windows with a view of the cliffs rising vertically from the water. Wooden tables and ferns dangling from the ceiling lend the place a trattoria-like feel. It serves generous fish platters *(parrillada de pescado)* and a great three-course menu including a drink for an unbeatable 9 euros! *Closed Tue | on the harbour pier | tel. 928 89 85 81 | €–€€*

> **INSIDER TIP**
> Great simple food!

AROUND PUERTO DE LAS NIEVES

🔟 AGAETE
2km / 2 mins east of Puerto de las Nieves on the local road

The pretty village (pop. 6,000) is situated at the end of a fertile sunny valley. Small streets that wind through a labyrinth of tightly packed houses start from the plaza opposite the church *Iglesia de la Concepción (admission free | ask inside for the key)*. The left-hand nave has a painting of the *Virgin of the Snow* by 16th-century Flemish master *Joos van Cleve*. There is also a lovely flower garden, *El Huerto de las Flores (closed Sun/Mon | admission 1.50 euros)*. Original souvenirs can be found at *Jabones Artesanos Jacaranda (C/ Lago 6 | Agaete | tel. 677 51 53 31)* who manufacture soaps from aloe vera, cactus fruits and goat's milk. *C–D2*

THE NORTH

🟧 VALLE DE AGAETE

12km / 20 mins southeast of Puerto de las Nieves via the GC 231

From Agaete, there is a valley where orange and lemon trees grow, and which stretches inland for 7km. At the end of the valley, there are narrow tracks up to the Tamadaba forest where you can go hiking. But before that, you'll pass *Maipéz (Apr-Sept Tue-Sun 10am-6pm, Oct-Mar 10am-5pm | admission 3 euros, combined ticket with other archaeological sites 10 euros)*, an archaeological park with 700 burial mounds in lava slag. Paths lead through the black terrain, which creates a strong contrast to the green of the valley – and again and again, you'll have lovely views, the best ones from the museum at the highest point! In addition, you can learn interesting facts about the ritual practices of the indigenous people.

> **INSIDER TIP**
> **Walking on lava**

Even further up into the valley, in *San Pedro*, you can visit the coffee plantations. At the romantic *Finca La Laja (daily 10am-5pm | 6 euros/pers including wine and coffee tasting (min. 2 people) | tel. 628 92 25 88 | bodega losberrazales.com | San Pedro | ⓘ 1.5 hrs)*, you will find out how beans that start out red are turned into aromatic black coffee. Incidentally, the house red and white wine label Los Berrazales is excellent and is served in a lovely garden setting. *▥ D2*

WHERE TO STAY IN THE NORTH

HISTORIC HACIENDA

Like a film set in the middle of a banana plantation, the *Hacienda del Buen Suceso (18 rooms | Arucas | GC 330, Km4.2 | tel. 928 62 29 45 | haciendabuensuceso.com | €€)* offers plenty of space for dreaming. Enjoy the view from the green terraces, take a leisurely swim in the pool, or relax in the on-site spa.

The pride of the village of Agaete

THE CENTRE

WILD GORGES & PRECIPITOUS PEAKS

Many people forget that the *cumbre*, as the island's mountainous area is called, reaches heights of almost 2,000m. On average, the temperature on Pico de las Nieves, the highest spot on Gran Canaria, is 10–20°C lower than on the coast; it is called the "snowy peak" for a reason. While holidaymakers make sure they've packed plenty of T-shirts and shorts, those living in the mountains always have a woollen hat and thick jacket close at hand between December and February.

Hiker at the Roque Nublo

Life in this rough environment is not easy. The barren, rugged *cumbre* seems a dangerous place. And when dark clouds move across and give the rocks and ridges a threatening air, it is easy to understand how the poet Miguel de Unamuno thought of this as a *tempestad petrificada*, a "petrified storm". The weather has carved canyons into the bedrock, but there are also upland plains as flat as pancakes. Reservoirs and sparse pine forests provide the odd bit of green. Mountain villagers go about their business at a gentle pace.

THE CENTRE

San Pedro

8 Pinar de Tamadaba ★

11km, 15 mins

Caldera Pinos de Gálda

Artenara
p.

24km, 1 hr

5 Puerto de la Aldea de San Nicolás

Tejeda ★
p. 83

Roque Bentayga
○ La Solana

● **La Aldea de San Nicolás**
p. 78

6 Barranco de la Aldea

4 Cactualdea

3 Güigüi

40km, 1½ hrs

13 Embalse Cueva de las Niñ

Embalse de Soria **14**

15 Embal de Ch

2 Playa de Tasarte

● **Mogán**
p. 76

1 Playa de Veneguera

MARCO POLO HIGHLIGHTS

★ **ARTENARA**
A cave village at a dizzying height ➤ p. 79

★ **PINAR DE TAMADABA**
The trade winds sweep gently through the island's largest pine forest
➤ p. 81

★ **PICO DE LAS NIEVES**
Magnificent panoramic views from Gran Canaria's highest peak ➤ p. 83

★ **TEJEDA**
This mountain village has been nominated as one of the most beautiful places in Spain ➤ p. 83

★ **ROQUE NUBLO**
Fantastic views on a hike to the Cloud Rock ➤ p. 85

★ **LA FORTALEZA**
A fortress in the rocks – Guanche retreat with spectacular views ➤ p. 89

Map of Gran Canaria (Eastern & Southern)

- Tafira Baja
- Teror
- Valleseco
- Santa Brígida
- Vega de San Mateo
- Valsequillo
- ● **Cruz de Tejeda** p.82
- ● **Telde**
- **9** Degollada de Becerra
- **Roque Nublo** ★
- **10 Pico de las Nieves** ★
- **Tyacata** p.85
- Urbanización Ojos de Garza
- **21** Guayadeque
- ● **San Bartolomé de Tirajana** p.87
- **22** Ingenio
- ● **Santa Lucía** p.88
- ● **Agüimes** p.90
- Fataga **16**
- El Sitio de Arriba
- **19 La Fortaleza** ★
- El Sitio de Abajo
- **17** Camel Safari Park La Baranda
- Vecindario
- Arinaga **20**
- **18** Necrópolis de Arteara
- San Agustín
- OCÉANO ATLÁNTICO
- Maspalomas
- Playa del Inglés
- Meloneras

5 km / 3.11 mi

MOGÁN

📍 *C6* **In the village of Mogán, which is where the reach of the tourists ends, you can immerse yourself in Gran Canaria's mountain world!**

The *Barranco de Mogán* stretches 12km inland from the coast. Drive up on the GC 200 through this fertile valley, past tiny villages surrounded by orange and lemon groves. Sleepy Mogán (pop. 700) is situated at 300m. It has a restored windmill, the *Molino de Viento (admission free)*, and curious stacks of objects of daily life, such as irons, cans and cups – some piled as high as a house – all remnants of the village parade. Higher up in the village are a pretty church square and houses surrounded by lavish gardens. You can get something to eat in the restaurants on main road or at the rustic *Acaymo (closed Mon | €€)*, which has a terrace, or at *Casa Enrique (open daily | €€)*.

AROUND MOGÁN

🏖 PLAYA DE VENEGUERA
18km / 40 mins southwest of Mogán via the GC 200/205
One of the few unspoilt beaches, Playa de Veneguera is 700m wide and covered in gravel. On your way back, stop at *Las Cañadas (GC-200, Km52.1 | tel. 928 94 35 90 | €€)*, a restaurant and grill with an ethno-museum and a 🎭 petting zoo | 📍 *B6*

🏖 PLAYA DE TASARTE
27km / 35 mins west of Mogán via the GC 200/206
Few people frequent this cove of dark sand and gravel, which is accessible via a narrow lane that eventually becomes a sand track. However, the food is delicious at *La Oliva (Tue–Sun 10am–6pm | tel. 928 89 43 58 | €€)*, a terraced restaurant. Especially good is the freshly caught fish, and paella at the weekend. | 📍 *B6*.

THE CENTRE

The restored windmill is one of several attractions in Mogán

3 GÜIGÜI

24km / 30 mins northwest of Mogán via the GC 200/204, then on foot

Gran Canaria's most remote beaches, *Güigüi Grande* ("large") and *Güigüi Chico* ("small"), are among the island's most beautiful coves. The surf along the west coast washes light-coloured sand onto the steep, forbidding land. Together with the gorge further inland, these coves are nature reserves, aiming to protect the unspoilt character of the region for future generations. Needless to say, the inaccessible location comes at a price: it takes fit hikers 2½ hours to reach the beaches from the hamlet of *Tasartico* over a mountain pass in the blazing sun. And don't forget the return journey takes just as long! Make sure you get good directions before setting out. A cliff casts its shadow over the 300-m long Güigüí Grande; the 600-m-long beach at Güigüí Chico follows behind a rocky ledge. It is only possible to move between the two beaches at low tide. There are no sanitary facilities and no way of getting help in a hurry should there be an accident. If you plan a day trip (don't forget sturdy shoes, food, water and sun protection), make sure you know the times of the tides. *A5*

LA ALDEA DE SAN NICOLÁS

LA ALDEA DE SAN NICOLÁS

(▭ B4) **This village stretches across a wide valley which is surrounded by high mountains.**

La Aldea de San Nicolás is the most isolated town on the island. Until recently, the only way to get to it from the north was via a spectacular yet tricky road along the cliffs. Falling rocks caused ths road to close; instead, a new tunnel-and-bridge road has been built using 100 million euros of EU funding with the aim of reducing the distance to "civilisation".

From afar, you will get an idea of how most of the 8,000 inhabitants make their living. Sheets of plastic, the size of football pitches, cover the landscape in a graphic pattern. This creates a microclimate that makes it possible to harvest tomatoes several times a year. La Aldea de San Nicolás itself is not the most attractive town imaginable, but the small plaza by the church is a pleasant spot.

EATING & DRINKING

EL ALBERCÓN

Halfway between the town centre and the harbour, chef Johannes serves **fantastic, freshly pressed fruit juice in his garden restaurant**. The tapas servings are generous too. *Open daily | C/ Albercón 4 | tel. 607 94 34 29 | €–€€*

INSIDER TIP: Organic shakes among the cacti

AROUND LA ALDEA DE SAN NICOLÁS

4 CACTUALDEA

5km / 7 mins south of La Aldea via the GC 200

You can admire 100,000 cacti and other desert plants while strolling through the "Cactus Village". *Daily 10am–5pm | admission 6.50 euros | tel. 928 89 12 28. | ▭ B4*

5 PUERTO DE LA ALDEA DE SAN NICOLÁS

5km / 5 mins northwest of La Aldea via the GC 200

It's fun to stroll along the promenade in this tiny harbour village and it's a great place to watch the ⚑ sunset. The promenade runs between the stony beach and a small, dense palm and pine tree forest with picnic tables in the shade that are used by Canarians at the weekend. The terrace restaurants have sea views, but the fish there is usually of inferior quality – the attitude seems to be: "tourists usually only come once, so anything'll do".

The promenade ends at the large breakwater that protects the moored fishing boats from the waves. There is an information centre in a former warehouse, offering advice on excursions around the region. *▭ A–B4*

THE CENTRE

6 BARRANCO DE LA ALDEA

30km / 1 hr northeast of La Aldea via the GC 210

If you want to leave civilisation behind, take the GC 210 from La Aldea de San Nicolás to Artenara. What is almost certainly Gran Canaria's least-travelled road is 30km long and in many places so narrow that two cars can't pass. The road starts in the centre of town (ask for *dirección Artenara*) and winds its way up to an altitude of 1,300m.

The gorge seems to have come right out of a Wild West film. The rock faces loom ever closer to the road, which winds up through a series of hairpin bends, passing reservoirs that store rainwater. Just before you reach a tunnel, you will be taken aback by your first glimpse of the monumental panorama of the *cumbre*. The scene is dominated by Gran Canaria's two major landmarks: the monoliths *Roque Bentayga* (on the left) and *Roque Nublo* (on the right).

> **INSIDER TIP**
> **Between heaven and earth**

At Km18.7 is a restored mill – after so many bends, this is a great place for a picnic and the views are fabulous.

The GC 216 road enters *Pinar de Tamadaba* pine forest to the left at an altitude of almost 1,200m. However, keep to the right and reach Artenara in ten minutes. *B3–D4*

ARTENARA

D3 Gran Canaria's highest mountain village, ★Artenara, is full of inhabited caves: museums and chapels, restaurants and shops – all hewn out of the rock.

The prehispanic Canarians knew that the caves had a unique microclimate – cool in summer and warm in winter. This is especially advantageous in Artenara which, at an altitude of 1,270m, can get pretty cold in winter.

SIGHTSEEING

MUSEO DE LAS CASAS CUEVAS

The multi-storey cave dwelling is as charmingly furnished as if Señor Santiago Arranda, a farmer and the last owner, was still living there:

Cactualdea: watch out for spikes!

ARTENARA

freshly made beds in alcoves, a living room with family photos and a crucifix, a delightful kitchen, a ceramics workshop and a weaving mill. Canaries twitter everywhere, closely watched by stray cats. It is also home to the tourist office. *Daily 10am–5pm | admission free | C/ Párroco Domingo Báez | 30 mins*

VIRGEN DE LA CUEVITA

The chapel of the Virgin of the Small Cave is a room of approximately 80m² that has been chiselled into a vertical drop. Bench-like niches have been cut out of the rock, and the raised oriel was reserved for village dignitaries. The original confessional, the altar and the pulpit were all made from volcanic rock. *Open 24 hrs | walk or drive up the steep track from the plaza*

The Virgen de la Cuevita chapel was hewn out of volcanic rock

IGLESIA DE SAN MATÍAS

The centre of the village is at the point where the church steeples rise towards the sky. Inside, the barrel vaults and fine wooden coffers in Canarian pine are worth a look. You'll also like the 20th-century frescoes by Jesús Arencibia. *Open daily*

EATING & DRINKING

CASA DEL CORREO

This restaurant run with love by two Canarian women and located across from the church serves up a delicious *garbanzada* (chickpea stew). *Closed Mon | Plaza de San Matías 7 | tel. 622 15 33 31 | €*

THE CENTRE

MESÓN MIRADOR LA CILLA
After traversing a 50-m tunnel, you will have the world at your feet. There are views across the rugged Caldera de Tejeda as far as the basalt rocks of Roque Bentayga and Roque Nublo. The food – Canarian, with lots of meat – is almost of secondary importance. *Open daily | Camino de la Cilla 8 | tel. 928 66 62 27 | FB: Restaurante La Cilla | €€*

SHOPPING

ARTE GAIA
INSIDER TIP — Shop local
The cave shop sells food, cosmetics and crafts made in Gran Canaria – and you can also enjoy a glass of wine on the terrace. *Daily 11am–5pm | Camino de la Cilla 17 | arte-gaia.com*

AROUND ARTENARA

7 CALDERA PINOS DE GÁLDAR
9km / 12 mins northeast of Artenara via the GC 21
Drive north from Artenara, and you'll soon find yourself in greener countryside. Seven kilometres along the GC-21 towards Teror, you'll pass the vast crater *(caldera)* of an extinct volcano. The steep slopes are covered in *picón*, tiny lava stones, and ash, and descend evenly to the bottom of the crater. Enjoy the views into the depths from a viewing platform. *E3*

8 PINAR DE TAMADABA ★
11km / 15 mins northwest of Artenara via the GC 216
The largest forested area on Gran Canaria is almost exclusively made up of *Pinus canariensis*, the Canarian pine. This tall tree has adapted itself perfectly to survive in the volcanic environment. The thick bark that once protected the trunk like a fireproof jacket from the heat of the falling ash, does the same today against forest fires. In this way, even trees that are completely singed on the outside are still alive inside and come into leaf again after a blaze (for example the one in 2019). The thin, green, very long needles draw water from the passing trade winds that then drips to the ground. The long lichens hanging like an old man's beard from the branches on the northern slopes where the trade winds are strongest are especially noteworthy. They are nourished entirely by the clouds.

The ring road GC-216 runs up to the forest, with barbecue ovens, tables and benches at the northern tip being restored from 2021. Hiking trails lead off to the right and left.

When the weather is clear, it is worth stopping on the north side and following the marked path to *Risco Faneque*, which is one of the world's highest cliffs with a view down on the coast. It's a two-hour round trip. It is said that, after the Spaniards had conquered the island, many indigenous people jumped to their death from these cliffs. *C–D3*

INSIDER TIP — Mind your step!

CRUZ DE TEJEDA

Cruz de Tejeda: starting point for wonderful mountain hikes

CRUZ DE TEJEDA

E4 **At an altitude of 1,490m, Cruz de Tejeda is the most important road junction in the** *cumbre***.**

From here, roads fan out to all parts of the island. Although it's not a village as such, it is a very popular day-trip destination and you will find a surprising number of restaurants in a small area. The mountain views from the terrace of the *Parador Hotel* are spectacular.

EATING & DRINKING

ASADOR DE YOLANDA
Hearty food in a rustic atmosphere, including grilled meats, but many people only stop by for a glass of wine or a cup of coffee. *Daily from 9am | tel. 928 66 62 76 | asadoryolanda.com | €€*

AROUND CRUZ DE TEJEDA

9 DEGOLLADA DE BECERRA
4km / 5 mins south of Cruz de Tejeda via the GC 150, Km2.4
It's worth stopping at this *mirador* on the way to the Pico de las Nieves. The views around the rugged *Tejeda* caldera are tremendous. *E4*

THE CENTRE

🔟 PICO DE LAS NIEVES ⭐ 🏁
10km / 15 mins southeast of Cruz de Tejeda via the GC 150

At an altitude of 1,949m, the "Snowy Peak" is Gran Canaria's highest mountain … and in winter it occasionally snows here. The panoramic views from the road across large sections of the island are breathtaking. On the opposite side of the mountain top, the *Pozo de la Nieve Grande (near the antennas)*, you might even be able to see the southern tip of Fuerteventura on particularly clear days. It is not possible to climb to the peak itself because it is part of a restricted military area. 📖 *E4*

TEJEDA

(📖 *E4*) **The terraced mountain village of ⭐ Tejeda (pop. 2,400; alt. 1,050m) has been named one of the "prettiest villages in Spain". Let's see if you agree.**

It is situated on several hills and plateaus on the sunny south side of the massive *Caldera de Tejeda*. Following traditional Canarian style, the whitewashed houses have green shutters and wooden balconies. Lanes, steps and squares surround the church. Walking down the main road is like strolling along a promenade. Opposite is the impressive *Roque Bentayga*, and the *Roque Nublo* is not far away. Tejeda is at its liveliest at the beginning of February, when the village is framed by a sea of pink and white flowers, and thousands flock here for the almond blossom festival.

SIGHTSEEING

CENTRO DE PLANTAS MEDICINALES

Of all the small exhibition centres in Tejeda, this is the most interesting: a large number of the plants grown in the garden in front of the greyish-brown stone building are dried to make *infusiones* (herbal teas) – try a cup while you are there! A real highlight is the 19th-century chemist's shop, with its beautiful porcelain jars, old scales and weights, that was "transplanted" here in its entirety. *Tue–Sun 10am–3.30pm | admission 3 euros | C/ Párroco Rodríguez Vega 10 |* ⏱ *30 mins*

EATING & DRINKING

ASADERO EL ALMENDRO

First-class meat dishes, grilled to perfection, plus spectacular mountain scenery. *Daily from 11am | Av. de los Almendros 20, Ctra GC 60, Km1.5 | tel. 928 66 65 25 | FB: asadorelalmendro | €–€€*

CASA DE LOS CAMINEROS

The concept of this restaurant is quite original – tapas with ham and cheese, salads and stews are served in an artistic cafeteria-style ambience with an open view into the studio of artist/cook Armando Gil. *Closed Tue | Av. de los Almendros 5 | at the upper village road, direction Cruz de Tejeda | tel. 609 16 6961 | €*

INSIDER TIP: A feast for the senses

TEJEDA

GAYFA
The Canarian home-made cooking tastes even better on the scenic terrace. Try their stew *(potaje)* or simply enjoy a cold drink. *Daily from 7am | C/ Hernández Guerra 17 | tel. 928 66 62 30 | FB: Bar-Restaurante Gayfa |* €–€€

SHOPPING

DULCERÍA NUBLO TEJEDA
This confectioner on the main street has been here for generations and is well known all over the island. *Mantecados*, *piñones* and *mazapán*, Tejeda's marzipan pastries, will tempt anyone with a sweet tooth. Popular is *bienmesabe* ("it tastes good to me"), an almond mousse made with honey and lemon – a veritable feast for the senses. *Daily 9am–8pm | C/ Hernández Guerra 15*

INSIDER TIP: Almond delicacies

SPORT & ACTIVITIES

If you live in the middle of the mountains, you're not far from the starting points for Gran Canaria's loveliest walks and hikes. How about a panorama trip to *Roque Nublo*? Or a hike along the dramatic break-off edge of the Caldera de Tejeda to the neighbouring village of *Artenara*? It's a good idea to take a detailed hiking guidebook with you.

You can buy traditional pastries at the Dulcería Nublo Tejeda

THE CENTRE

AROUND TEJEDA

11 ROQUE BENTAYGA
7km / 12 mins southwest of Tejeda via the GC 60

The 1,412m basalt monolith was sacred to the Guanche people – and no wonder: it soars strikingly above the ridge to the southwest of Tejeda like a fossilised exclamation mark. The Guanches held sacrificial ceremonies on the site at the foot of the mountain, which can be reached from the car park *(daily 10am–5pm)*. You can find out more in the small *Visitor Centre (Centro de Interpretación, Tue–Sun 9.30am–4.30pm | admission free | tel. 928 47 48 51 | grancanaria.com/bentayga).* ⌘ *D4*

AYACATA

⌘ *E4* **This small village on the southern side of the *cumbre* is famous for the almond blossom in January and February.**

Down-to-earth home-style cooking and many day trippers can be found in the pleasant *Casa Melo* restaurant *(open daily | tel. 928 17 22 61 | €)* – but ask for the price before you order! From here you can continue in whichever direction you prefer: northbound to *Tejeda* (GC 60), eastbound to the *Roque Nublo* (GC 600), southbound to *Maspalomas* (GC 60) and westbound to *Mogán* (GC 605). The narrow GC 605 road leads from Ayacata to a dreamy landscape of deep gorges, steep ridges, extensive pine forests and reservoirs.

AROUND AYACATA

12 ROQUE NUBLO ★
3km / 5 mins northeast of Ayacata via the GC 600

Gran Canaria's most famous landmark soars into the sky like a giant's axe. The 1,813-m-high block of basalt, rises 80m above a flat-topped mountain. As was the case with Roque Bentayga, the indigenous Canarians considered this "Cloud Rock" to be a sacred place. It can be reached in 45 minutes by following a winding path from the car park (see p. 124).

Two plateaus reveal glorious panoramic views over large sections of the island as far as Tenerife. Also take a look at Roque Nublo's two companions, *Fraile and Rana*. Depending on where you are, and with a little imagination, you will recognise in the rocks the profile of a monk *(fraile)* and a frog *(rana)*. If you drive a few minutes further uphill, you will reach one of the Canarios' favourite picnic areas at *Llanos de la Pez*. The barbecues and picnic tables are usually occupied at weekends; the locals like to come here with their families and relax in the beautiful landscape. This is a perfect opportunity for sociable tourists to get to know Canarian people. ⌘ *E4*

AROUND AYACATA

🔟 EMBALSE CUEVA DE LAS NIÑAS 🏳
9km / 15 mins southwest of Ayacata via the GC 605

After winter rains, the "Reservoir of the Girls' Cave" is seen at its very best: the mirror-smooth surface is surrounded by plenty of greenery, ducks glide over the water and goats come to drink. It's the perfect spot for an extended picnic on rustic stone tables. The necessary barbecue ovens, water, loos and sometimes a snack stall are provided. By contrast, the lake often dries up in summer, when it becomes a loamy pine-shaded area. *D5*

🔟 EMBALSE DE SORIA 🏳
15km / 30 mins southwest of Ayacata via the GC 605 and GC 505

Gran Canaria's biggest reservoir is framed by majestic palms. On its southern edge is the hamlet of *Soria* and the *Casa Fernando (closed Sun | tel. 928 17 23 46 | €)*. This restaurant has its own terrace and serves hearty Canarian food in a rustic atmosphere. From Ayacata, drive towards Mogán, then turn left onto a narrower road leading to El Barranquillo Andrés. Finally, turn left to Soria. *D5*

Among pine forests and rocks high above the Cueva de las Niñas reservoir

THE CENTRE

SAN BARTOLOMÉ DE TIRAJANA

(Ⓜ E5) **Don't be surprised if, instead of the official name San Bartolomé, you often read or hear *Tunte*, a name that goes back to the Guanches and means "the place of the people".**

As you stroll along the lanes, you'll be rewarded with fabulous views of the gigantic *Caldera de Tirajana*, shaped over eons by the weather and strong winds. The village (pop. 4,000) is dominated by the pretty 18th-century church that is dedicated to Santiago, the patron saint of Spain. In fact, he can be seen twice, wielding his sword and on horseback, in the aisle on the right. Don't miss the beautifully carved wooden ceilings in the three-aisled, Mudéjar-style church.

You should also head next door to the *Casa Yánez (Mon–Fri 9am–1pm | admission free | C/ Antonio Yánez 1)*, an ethnological museum that depicts Canarian life on large farms a long time ago. In the reconstructed little shop you will also find the tourist information office. Here, visitors are offered a taster of the local fruit liqueur *mejunje ¡Salud!*

> **INSIDER TIP**
> Taste the fruit

EATING & DRINKING

LA PANERA DE TUNTE
This bakery in San Bartolomé de Tirajana not only sells delicious sandwiches *(bocadillos)*, but also local wine. You can eat the inexpensive snacks on the roadside terrace. *Open daily | C/ Reyes Católicos | €*

SHOPPING

BODEGA LAS TIRAJANAS
Try the wines of the south. Book in advance for a guided tour including wine tasting *(6–9 euros/person). Mon–Fri 10am–4pm, Sat/Sun 10am–2pm | C/ Las Lagunas | tel. 628 21 66 83 | bodegaslastirajanas.com*

AROUND SAN BARTOLOMÉ DE TIRAJANA

15 EMBALSE DE CHIRA
13km / 20 mins southwest of San Bartolomé via the GC 60/604
The reservoir has a magnificent setting in a depression below a dense pine forest. A twisty road that offers many wonderful views of the countryside leads down to it. Two simple bars guarantee that day trippers don't go hungry or thirsty. *D–E5*

16 FATAGA
9km / 15 mins south of San Bartolomé via the GC 60
The village, hidden deep in the valley, has remained an intact ensemble of white houses with red-tiled roofs, a small plaza and narrow, winding streets. In the middle of an oasis of palm trees 1km to the north a comfortable country hotel has been established on a 200-year-old farm. They serve Canarian cuisine in the restaurant on the terrace *(open daily | tel. 928 17 22 44 | €-€€)*. *E6*

17 CAMEL SAFARI PARK LA BARANDA
12km / 20 mins south of San Bartolomé via the GC 60
Two kilometres south of Fataga you can join a 20-minute "safari". However, it's just as much fun to just look around and enjoy a freshly pressed juice! *Mon–Sat 8am–6pm | 30-minute ride 22 euros, including lunch 34 euros, children half price | tel. 928 79 86 80 | camelsafarigrancanaria.com | E–F6*.

18 NECRÓPOLIS DE ARTEARA
13km / 25 mins south of San Bartolomé via the GC 60/601
Thousands of years ago, a rock avalanche descended above the palm oasis of Arteara. The indigenous people used this stony desert as a burial site. Today, the necropolis is an archaeological park and can be visited on a circular trail. **The silence and rugged rockiness of this place create a special atmosphere.** *INSIDER TIP: A magical place* If you don't want to approach via the 1km, narrow village lane, park the car at the entrance to the village and walk. The fauna and flora of the oasis are explained on information boards, and the flower-clad houses are charming. *Tue–Sun 10am–2pm, closed July/Aug | admission 4 euros, combined ticket with other archaeological sites 10 euros | 1 hr | E–F6*

SANTA LUCÍA

(F5) **This quiet village at the eastern edge of the Caldera de Tirajana, the vast caldera in the southern mountains, is just beautiful.**

The houses and farms lie in the midst of small palm groves and avenues of tall eucalyptus trees scattered across the wide semicircle formed by

THE CENTRE

the slopes. There is an impressive church from the early 19th century in the centre of the village; its tower crowned with a minaret is reminiscent of a mosque. In front of the church, a sculpture pays homage to "matriarchy". Sit down on the bench next to this "strong woman" and have your picture taken! Along the road there are a number of restaurants and small shops selling oranges and lemons, pickled olives and locally made goat's cheese.

EATING & DRINKING

EL MIRADOR

The best views of the valley's vast expanse are from this restaurant. Goat is a particular delicacy here, especially when enjoyed with a glass of local red wine. *Open daily | C/ Maestro Enrique Hernández 5 | tel. 928 79 80 05 | FB: Restaurante El Mirador de Santa Lucía | €–€€*

The interior of Santa Lucía's church

AROUND SANTA LUCÍA

19 LA FORTALEZA ★

6km / 8 mins south of Santa Lucía via the GC 65/651

The huge fortress mountain below Santa Lucía (accessible via the GC-651, signposted) was used as a retreat by indigenous people during the Conquista. They lived in a huge cave that is open in both directions and, if you like, you can climb up to it (no torch required). Having walked through the cave and reached its other end, you will be rewarded with spectacular views of the surrounding gorges. The attractive Visitor Centre, a short distance down the road, tells you about what happened in La Fortaleza in 1483. On your way there, visit the viewing platform of the tiny *La Sorrueda* reservoir. When filled with water, it resembles an emerald that has been thrown into the landscape. *Tue–Sun 10am–5pm | admission 4 euros, children aged 5–12 2 euros | Hoya del Rábano 48, GC 651, Km1.9 | lafortaleza.es | 1 hr | F5*

AGÜIMES

(G5) **After careful restoration, Agüimes (pop. 14,000) is now one of the prettiest towns of the Canary Islands.**

The winding streets are lined with ochre-coloured houses and your footsteps echo over the cobblestones.

Cave restaurant in Guayadeque

Every now and then you will stumble upon quaint statues, snug corners and pretty squares as you explore this old bishop's seat.

SIGHTSEEING

IGLESIA DE SAN SEBASTIÁN
The church, built in 1796, seems as mighty as a cathedral and has impressive baroque sculptures inside. *C/ Sebastián Parer*

MUSEO DE HISTORIA
The island's history is retold in a very "picturesque" way in this former bishop's palace. This includes witchcraft in the Canaries. Videos show Voodoo practices, and you can learn a lot about fertility-promoting herbs. *Tue-Sun 9am-5pm | admission 2.50 euros | FB: MuseoHistoriaAguimes | 30 mins*

EATING & DRINKING

TASCA MI PUEBLO
Enjoy the small dishes in this rustic bar; there's no charge for the view of the church square. *Closed Mon | C/ Progreso 50 | tel. 605 80 25 61 | €€*

AROUND AGÜIMES

20 ARINAGA
10km / 10 mins southeast of Agüimes via the GC 100

"Do I really want to go there?" you may ask yourself as you drive through the sprawling industrial sites. But once you've made it to the coast, you won't regret it: there is a 4-km-long promenade along tiny gravel coves that ends to the north at the historic lime kilns. Dine at the fish restaurant *Hornos del Cal (daily*

INSIDER TIP — By the ocean

THE CENTRE

from noon | Av. Playa de Arinaga | €€) right beside the sea. Incidentally, the water near the coast is ideal for diving – as is suggested by the oversized fish sculptures. One kilometre away, the lighthouse, *Faro de Arinaga*, is worth a detour (see p. 122)! H6

21 GUAYADEQUE

10km / 12 mins northwest of Agüimes via the GC 103

The *Barranco de Guayadeque* is one of the narrowest, steepest and greenest gorges on Gran Canaria. Maybe that's the reason why the early Canarians settled here. There are hundreds of cave dwellings hidden in the lava stone – many of them still lived in today. A large number of burial sites full of bones and mummified bodies from the pre-Spanish period have been discovered in Guayadeque – a visitor centre tells the story of the thousand years the caves were used *(Museo de Sitio Guayadeque | Tue–Sat 9am–5pm, Sun 10am–6pm | admission 2.50 euros)*.

There is a cave chapel as well as several cave restaurants in the valley. The rustic *El Centro (daily noon-10pm | Cuevas Bermejas on the left, in the middle of the valley | tel. 928 17 21 45 | €)* is made up of a series of niches and narrow, winding corridors and serves local cuisine. The large restaurant *Tagoror (daily 10am–11pm | tel. 928 17 2013 | restaurantetagoror.com | €€)* at the end of the cul-de-sac is equally labyrinthine. F–G5

INSIDER TIP: Dine in a cave

22 INGENIO

3km / 5 mins north of Agüimes via the GC 100

Agüime's less impressive twin had its heyday during the sugar cane boom when the town was dominated by the many *ingenios* (sugar mills). There is a well-preserved press at the roundabout on the road to Carrizal. Ingenio is famous as a centre for Canarian embroidery. You can buy handmade items and admire a year-round nativity scene in the *Museo de Piedras y Artesanía Canaria (Mon–Sat 10am–6pm | visit to the nativity 1 euro | GC 100, at the end of the Las Mejías district)*. G5

WHERE TO STAY IN THE CENTRE

HIGH IN THE MOUNTAINS

In *Las Tirajanas* hotel *(60 rooms | C/ Oficial Mayor José Rubio | tel. 928 56 69 69 | hotelrurallastirajanas.com | €€–€€€)* you can enjoy magnificent panoramic views, an upmarket country house atmosphere and, on cloudy days, a cave-like spa (with indoor pool). They also offer free activities such as guided hikes.

CLOSE TO NATURE WITH A VIEW

Tejeda is home to the small but elegant *Fonda de la Tea* hotel *(12 rooms | C/ Ezequiel Sánchez 22 | tel. 928 66 64 22 | hotelfondadelatea.com | €€–€€€)*, which provides a comfortable base for tours into the mountains.

THE SOUTH COAST

SUN & SAND

The clouds brought in by the northeast trade winds seem to stop in their tracks when they hit the mountains. In the south the temperature is almost always 3–5°C higher than in the north, and the sun shines 350 days of the year.

However, the warm, dry climate is not the only attraction. The fantastic beaches and unique dunes of the Costa Canaria draw hundreds of thousands of holidaymakers to the island every year.

You are rarely on your own on Maspalomas beach!

Further west, on the Costa Mogán, steep cliffs rise out of the ocean. But even this area has been developed for tourism with man-made beaches and marinas. No matter how small, resorts have been squeezed onto the slopes in most of the bays along the coast. Now that more and more tourists are coming to the Canary Isles on holiday, a construction ban – supposed to restrict the number of beds in the area – has been officially lifted.

THE SOUTH COAST

MARCO POLO HIGHLIGHTS

★ **DUNAS DE MASPALOMAS**
A Saharan sensation next to the sea
➤ p. 103

★ **PALMITOS PARK**
An exotic experience in the hinterland
➤ p. 105

★ **LÍNEAS SALMÓN**
A cruise on an excursion boat offers a different view of the island ➤ p. 109

★ **BARRANCO DE ARGUINEGUÍN**
It plunges deep down into the valley and all the way up to the mountains and a reservoir ➤ p. 110

★ **COASTAL PROMENADE**
A stroll between Puerto Rico and Playa de Amadores reveals fantastic views of the Atlantic ➤ p. 111

★ **PUERTO DE MOGÁN**
Fishing and holiday village with a pretty harbour ➤ p. 112

Palmitos Park ★ 6
5 Finca Montecristo

Puerto de Mogán ★
p. 112
12 10 Tauro
Taurito
GC1
27km, 15 mins

8 Barranco de Arguineguín ★
12km, 15 mins

Playa del Cura 11
GC1
Playa de Amadores 9
Coastal promenade ★
Líneas Salmón ★
Puerto Rico
p. 110

7 Playa de la Verga
GC1

10km, 40 mins

Maspaloma
p. 10

Arguineguín
p. 108

Playa de Maspalomas

Melonera
p. 10

OCÉANO ATLÁNTICO

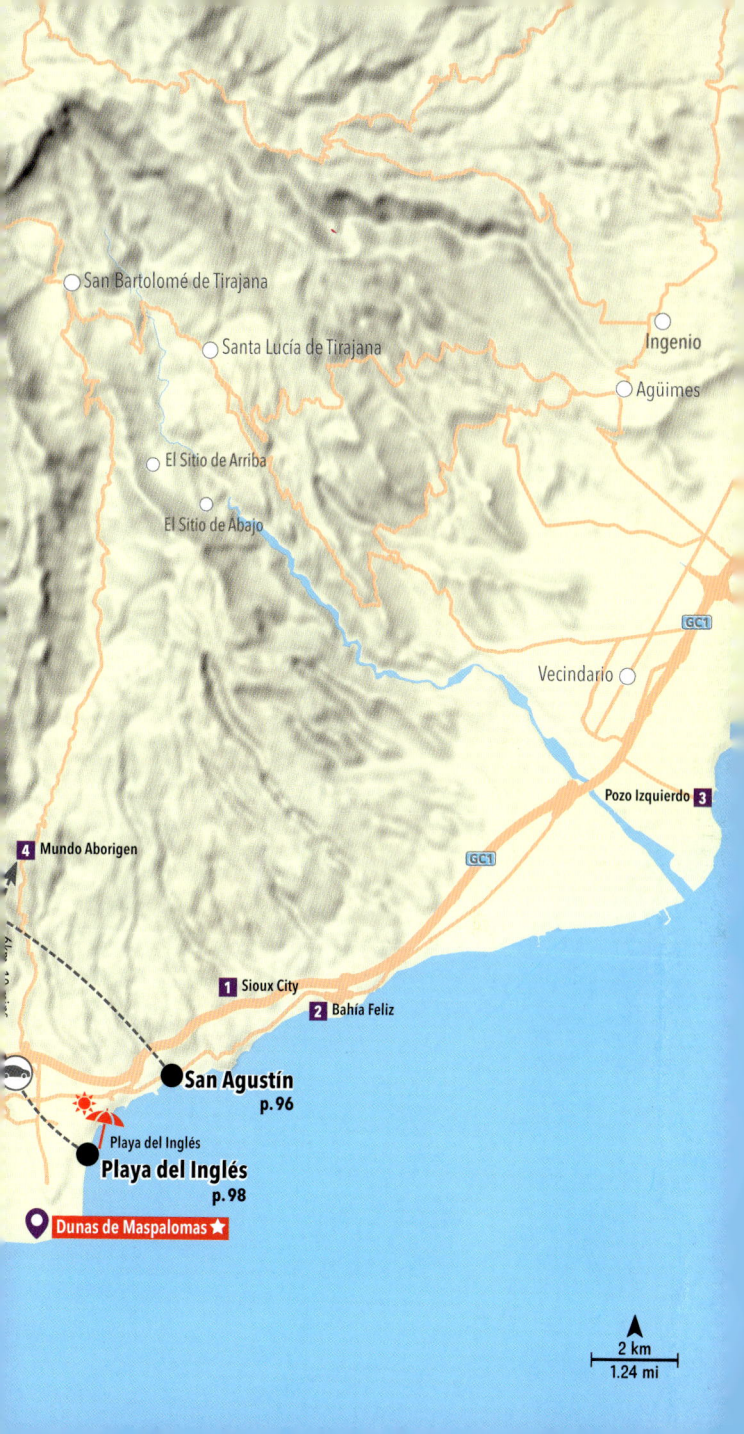

- San Bartolomé de Tirajana
- Santa Lucía de Tirajana
- Ingenio
- Agüimes
- El Sitio de Arriba
- El Sitio de Abajo
- Vecindario
- GC1
- Pozo Izquierdo **3**
- **4** Mundo Aborigen
- GC1
- **1** Sioux City
- **2** Bahía Feliz
- **San Agustín** p. 96
- Playa del Inglés
- **Playa del Inglés** p. 98
- Dunas de Maspalomas ★

2 km / 1.24 mi

SAN AGUSTÍN

(□ F8) **Everything is a little more relaxed and refined in San Agustín. In places, the precipitous coastline has ensured that the terraced bungalow complexes have magnificent sea views and are protected from the trade winds.**

Many hotels have been given a facelift and even the main throughroad has been modernised, but not yet the *Centro Comercial*. If you choose to stay in the newer sections on the slopes, you will still have panoramic views but it's further to go to the beach.

EATING & DRINKING

BAMIRA
Owners Anna and Herbert love to be inspired on their travels. **INSIDER TIP: Canarian globetrotters** Each season they revamp the menu according to their latest visit to foreign lands. When we last came to this restaurant, the scallops with sea urchin curry and the lamb fillet with palm honey were delicious. Quirky, yet elegant interior. *Closed Wed and from June to Sept | C/ Los Pinos 11 | Playa del Águila, 3.5km northeast of San Agustín | tel. 928 76 76 66 | bamira.com | €€€*

GREEK TAVERNA
Standing out in San Agustín's Centro Comercial (CC), this blue-and-white restaurant with a relaxed design serves Mediterranean classics. The *Taverna Meze* starters are delicious and ideal for sharing. The adjoining café opens at 8am. *Daily from 8am | CC San Agustín | tel. 928 76 67 85 | sabordegrecia.com | €€*.

SPORT & ACTIVITIES

DIVING CENTER NAUTICO
This diving centre picks you up from your hotel and takes you back after your dive. The taster course first teaches you the basics before instructing you in the hotel pool – and then you are off into the Atlantic! *C/ Los Jazmines 2 | tel. 928 77 02 00 | lopesan.com | €€*

BEACHES

Playa de las Burras ("donkey beach") is a 400m-long bay bordered by rocks on both sides and perfectly protected from the waves. There are sun loungers and parasols for hire but no sanitary facilities. *Playa de San Agustín* is an almost 900m beach of fine sand with only a few rocks here and there. It is bordered by steep cliffs on both sides that separate it from the Playa de las Burras to the west.

WELLNESS

THALASSO GLORIA
Be pampered in the gloriously relaxing 35°C waters of the **biggest thalassic spa and health centre on the Canary Islands**. **INSIDER TIP: In aqua veritas** Schedule a minimum of two hours to experience the various hydro-massage stations. There are

THE SOUTH COAST

It's not far to the beach from the bungalows in San Agustín

three pools, dozens of therapy facilities, trained staff and a fitness centre, and children are welcome, too. *Las Margaritas | San Agustín | tel. 928 76 56 89 | gloriapalaceth.com*

NIGHTLIFE

The nightlife takes place at the bars in the *Centro Comercial San Agustín*.

GORBEA CHILLOUT

Under the Bedouin tent on the roof of the hotel *Gloria Palace*, you can look across the skyline of San Agustín as you enjoy a refreshing cocktail. *Daily from 6pm | C/ Las Margaritas | gloriapalaceth.com*

AROUND SAN AGUSTÍN

1 SIOUX CITY
3km / 8 mins northeast of San Agustín via the GC 1

Actors on horseback re-enact scenes from the Wild West with wooden houses, a bank, sheriff's office and shops that look as if they have come straight out of a film, in this – somewhat outdated – Western town in a barranco near San Agustín. On Friday evenings at 8pm, there is a large barbecue and live music until midnight. Admission also includes drinks

PLAYA DEL INGLÉS

(*E-F8*) **The mega settlement of Playa del Inglés in the extreme south of the island is all about sand, sun and fun, popular with an international LGBT community.**

It has now almost completely fused with the neighbouring towns of San Agustín and Maspalomas, and there could be 100,000 or maybe even 120,000 beds for holidaymakers in the countless bungalow and holiday flat complexes. The labyrinth of streets in the Englishman's Beach" makes it difficult for anybody but insiders to find their way around. Tourist officials have realised that Playa del Inglés is in urgent need of a facelift. New green areas and the planned demolition of some buildings should make the holiday metropolis more attractive.

There is a promenade high up, parallel to the coast, with steps down to the long beach. The traffic-free *Avenida de Sargentos Provisionales* also goes to the playa via *Anexo II*, as the "food mile" with the vast (paying) car park and tourist information centre. Another access, this time across the super-hot sand on the beach, is from the *Ríu Palace Maspalomas* hotel: the views of the dunes from the lookout platform below the hotel are fabulous, especially just before sunrise. At sunset, buskers may provide you with some romantic music!

> **INSIDER TIP**
> Sights and sounds

at those events. *Tue–Sun 10am–4pm | admission 22 euros, barbecue 55 euros | Cañón del Aguila | exit: Playa del Aguila | tel. 928 76 29 82 | siouxcitypark.es. | F7*

2 BAHÍA FELIZ

5.5km / 10 mins northeast of San Agustín via the GC 1

The Moorish-style architecture of this holiday complex makes it something out of the ordinary. Many of the bungalows have small towers and domes. There is only one hotel, a small shopping centre and a few restaurants; but there are several surf schools, in particular the *Fanatic Boarders Center (fanatic-boarders center.com)*. Close to the resort is the *Gran Karting Club (daily 10am–9pm | cart 18 euros for 8 mins | exit the GC 500 at Km7)* with a 1,650m cirecular track and special tracks for children. *F8*

3 POZO IZQUIERDO

20km / 20 mins northeast of San Agustín via the GC 1/194

The access road is not pretty, and the place itself is no beauty either. But thanks to its strong winds, Pozo Izquierdo is Gran Canaria's windsurfing hotspot. The largest wind farm on the island is found in the area behind the beach. This is where you could also find one of the island's last salt evaporation ponds, the *Salina de Tenefé (advance booking only | tel. 928 75 97 06)*. Sea salt is harvested in 365 salt pans almost entirely with the use of the wind and sun. *H7*

THE SOUTH COAST

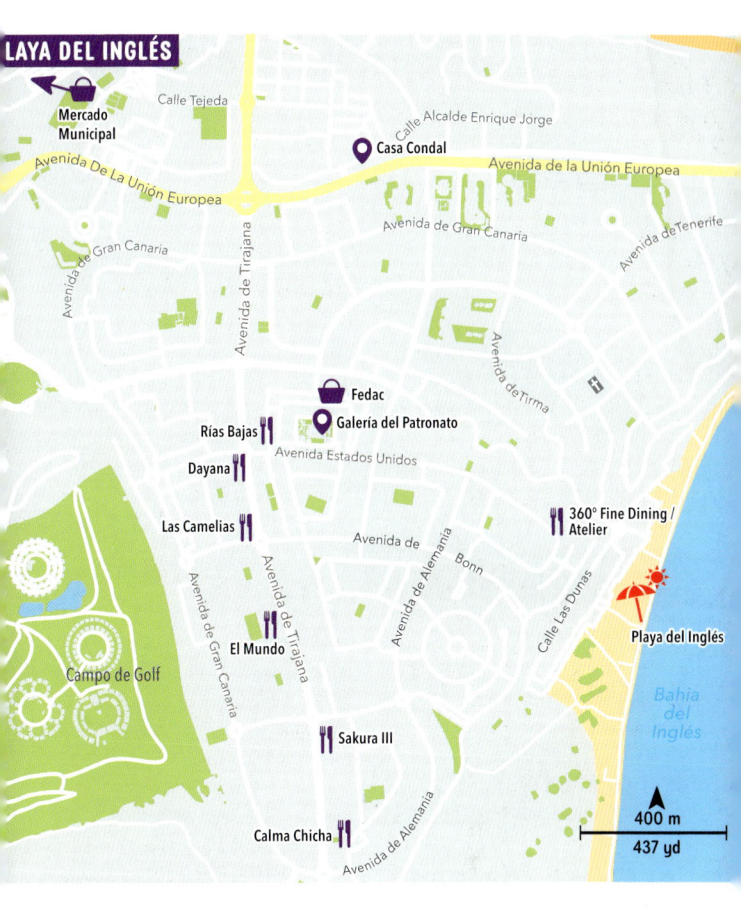

PLAYA DEL INGLÉS

SIGHTSEEING

CASA CONDAL
The museum in the "Count's House" tells the story of the island from its underwater birth to the present day. *C/ Marcial Franco 7-9 | San Fernando*

GALERÍA DEL PATRONATO
This neo-Canarian palace houses not just Gran Canaria's biggest (and arguably best) tourist information office, but also a gallery, showcasing local artists. The FEDAC arts and crafts shop also has a branch here (see p. 101). *Av. de España 1/Av. Estados Unidos, at the CC Yumbo | admission free*

EATING & DRINKING

360° FINE DINING / ATELIER
Cheeky design meets fine cuisine with 360° views over dunes and mountains. Enjoy the creative Canarian dishes

PLAYA DEL INGLÉS

served on the top floor of the 5-star *Bohemia Suites. Open daily | Av. Estados Unidos 25 | tel. 928 56 3400 | grancanaria-360.com | €€€*

A relaxed evening in Playa del Inglés

CALMA CHICHA

INSIDER TIP: Still waters run deep

The unassuming entrance to the "still waters" at the southern end of the Avenida is a gateway to a culinary oasis. This is fine dining. How about marinated tuna on a tomato consommé with strawberries and coriander foam? A nice, relaxed atmosphere. *Mon–Sat 7–10.30pm | Av. de Tirajana 4 | tel. 928 76 07 14 | restaurantecalmachicha.com | €€€*

DAYANA

Are you tired of fish and wrinkly potatoes? Then go to the Dayana where you can enjoy East Indian classics in a comfortable but elegant ambience. The menu includes vegetarian dishes like samosas and onion bhajis as well as chicken or lamb. *Tue–Sun 6pm–midnight | Av. Estados Unidos 56 | tel. 928 76 13 83 | restaurantedayana.com | €€*

EL MUNDO

This is fusion cooking: British black pudding meets Asian apple wontons or Thai veggie burgers team up with Greek tsatsiki. Reasonably priced set lunches. *Open daily | Av. de Tirajana | Edificio Tenesor | tel. 928 93 78 50 | FB: restaurante.mundo | €€*

LAS CAMELIAS

A place that has fed generations of tourists: in business since 1973, this restaurant offers a buffet with classic Canarian dishes ranging from vegetable stew *(potaje)*, fish and meat to crème caramel *(flan). Open daily | Av. de Tirajana 15 | tel. 928 07 47 20 | buffetlascamelias.com | €*

RÍAS BAJAS

A classic for fine (and expensive) seafood, unassuming on the outside but bright and elegant inside. You'll have to do without the sea views, though. *Open daily | Av. de Tirajana 26/Av. Estados Unidos | tel. 928 76 40 33 | FB: Rias Bajas Playa del Inglés | €€€*

THE SOUTH COAST

SAKURA III
Miso soup, seaweed salad, sushi, sashimi and various tofu creations – every traditional Japanese dish is served here. The restaurant is cheerfully decorated without any frills: the show kitchen in the centre lets you keep an eye on what the sushi master is up to. If you like things more intimate, you can eat seated on floor cushions in one of the niches. *Open daily | Av. de Tirajana 10 | tel. 928 76 55 27 | sakuracanarias.com | €€*

SHOPPING

FEDAC
The beautiful and useful Canarian crafts sold here are made from natural materials. They include ceramic and wooden bowls, leather and palm-frond bags and photo albums made of banana leaves. *Mon–Fri 10am–2pm and 4–7pm | Av. de España | Yumbo shopping centre (Tourist Information Office) | fedac.org*

MERCADO MUNICIPAL
Would you like to experience real Canarian daily life? The weekly market *(Wed and Sat 8am–2pm)* in the district of *San Fernando* has various food stalls as well as the usual fruit, vegetables, cheese and fish stalls. Also popular is the farmers' market *(every other Sun 8am–1pm)*.

SPORT & ACTIVITIES

MINI TREN
For a fun and nostalgic experience you can explore sprawling Playa del Inglés on a small 19th-century-style train. The e-locomotive pulls four small carriages behind it on its 30-minute sightseeing tour. You will find out all about the dunes and the lighthouse and chug past luxury hotels. *Daily 11am–noon and 2–5pm, every hour | 6 euros, children 3 euros | departure Av. de Italia | E7*

SKY DIVE
If you are brave enough, you can sky dive with an instructor from a small plane that takes off from the airfield near San Agustín. *Tel. 675 57 32 45 | approx. 250 euros | skydivegrancanaria.es*

WATER SPORT CENTER
The *water sport centre (tel. 659 44 00 08)* on *Anexo II* offers a variety of activities such as parasailing, paddle-surfing, jet-ski safaris, banana bus trips, kayak tours and kite surfing.

YUMBO
There is a large children's playground in the CC Yumbo shopping centre in Playa del Inglés with trampolines and bungees. The *Skyrider* is a ball that takes you 70m up into the sky! *Daily approx. 6–11pm | E8*

BEACHES

PLAYA DEL INGLÉS
The most famous beach on Gran Canaria is a stretch of sand approximately 8km long starting in San Agustín in the east and gently following the coastline as far as the

AROUND PLAYA DEL INGLÉS

Playa del Inglés: perennially popular

lighthouse on Playa de Maspalomas in the far south. At low tide, the beach is approximately 100m wide. It is clean and light coloured and ideal for long walks. There is an LGBT section of the beach and a section for nudists. On windy days, the rough surf and strong currents make this beach unsuitable, and not only for children! Keep an eye on the flags.

NIGHTLIFE

Later in the evening, the nightlife becomes more focused on the shopping centres (CCs). The *CC Yumbo*, with its cafés, pubs and bars is a hotspot for the gay scene. The no. 1 club is the elegant *Scala Heaven Theatre*: in-house DJs play house music almost every night. At *Ricky's Cabaret* there are extravagant transvestite shows, while live entertainment is on offer next door at the *Fiction (all clubs: Yumbo Center 3rd and 4th floor)*. At *Adonis* you get the best cocktails. Disco pub *Pachá (Av. Sargentos Provisionales 10 | pachagrancanaria.com)* has been popular for decades: 1,000m2 with four bars, fabulous lighting and loungers on the terrace for relaxing. They often have live music, fetish and champagne parties – and always a great atmosphere.

AROUND PLAYA DEL INGLÉS

4 MUNDO ABORIGEN

7km / 10 mins north of Playa del Inglés via the GC 60

THE SOUTH COAST

The drive through the Barranco de Fataga is an experience in itself. A brief excursion leads to the *Mirador de Yegua*: a fabulous viewing point of the gorge. About 1km before the mirador, you can visit the "World of the Aborigines", an open-air museum showcasing the life and traditions of the indigenous Canarians. Round stone houses, caves, burial sites and stables have been rebuilt in the spacious grounds. More than 100 life-size waxwork figures show everyday life and customs. *Daily 9am–6pm | admission 10 euros | approach via San Fernando | E7*

MASPALOMAS

(E8) This sprawling bungalow resort west of Playa del Inglés is bordered by the dunes, a lagoon and an ancient palm grove.

Everything is a little more upmarket in Maspalomas than in Playa del Inglés, except for the "food row" that runs parallel to the beach. The tall lighthouse from 1880 marks the border with Meloneras, although the two towns now seem to blend into one.

SIGHTSEEING

DUNAS DE MASPALOMAS ★

The dunes of Maspalomas are among the most magnificent landscapes of Gran Canaria. At their widest they reach 1.5km inland. The sand consists mainly of grains of coral and shells, worn down by the surf. You can walk through Gran Canaria's "Sahara desert", but only in the morning or from late afternoon, otherwise you may get sunstroke! The dunes are bordered to the west by the *Charca de Maspalomas*, a small lagoon of brackish and fresh water where herons, ducks, plovers, coots and many other birds stop over on their migrations (good information board on the promenade). Since the area became protected, many animals that were driven away during the construction boom have returned. It used to be possible to walk around the dunes as you pleased. However, the high level of development in recent decades has prevented the free movement of the wind-migrating dunes, which are also at risk of being slowly destroyed by the countless visitors. Now there are plans to restrict access to only one marked path through this desert of sand.

MASPALOMAS

EATING & DRINKING

CASA ANTONIO
This cosy gem with a view of the sea is tucked away in the centre of the small shopping promenade. Guests get to see the fish before it is cooked for them and pay for it by weight. Personal friendly service. *Open daily | tel. 928 14 11 53 | €-€€*

ESENCIA
The "essence" of Mediterranean cuisine is served in this top restaurant in a stylish retro pop-art ambience with weekly changing menus. The chef's signature dish is a lobster cocktail with fennel, apple, asparagus, blood orange and aniseed sprouts – an explosion of freshness on the tongue! *Mon, Wed and Fri/Sat 6.30–10pm | Hotel Seaside Palm Beach | Av. del Oasis 32 | tel. 928 72 10 32 | €€€*

SPORT & ACTIVITIES

AQUALAND
The Aqualand water park has dozens of water slides (all supervised); some are up to 150m long and you can ride down on rafts. Please note that children have to be at least 1–1.20m tall to use some of the slides. There are 5,300m2 of pool area, including a wave pool. You can drift leisurely through the grounds on a lazy river. The children's pools, with all kinds of water games and colourful fairy-tale figures, are popular. Please be aware that there are large areas of lawn and lush vegetation, and it's easy for parents to lose sight of their children! *Daily 10am–5pm | admission 26 euros, children under 10 17 euros, loungers, lockers, etc. for an extra fee | Barranco de Palmitos | approach via the GC 500 and GC 503, follow signs to Parques Temáticos on the right after 3km | aqualand.es/grancanaria*

CAMEL SAFARI
Above the lagoon *(Charca)*, on the edge of the dunes, is the camel station, the starting point for daily excursions. *Daily 9am–4pm | 30-min ride 12 euros, children 7 euros*

HOLIDAY WORLD
This leisure centre near Maspalomas has many attractions, and not just for kids: Ferris wheel, boat swings, merry-go-round, roller coaster, bumper cars and pirate ship, plus gaming machines from pinball to virtual car races. You pay separately for each attraction using a pre-paid chip card purchased on entry. *Sun–Thu 5–11pm, Fri/Sat 5pm–midnight | Av. Touroperador TUI/in the Campo Internacional | holidayworld-maspalomas.com*

BEACHES

PLAYA DE MASPALOMAS
sandy beach in front of the dunes is the western extension of Playa del Inglés. One section of the beach (with loungers and parasols) is reserved for nude bathing. The *balneario municipal* at the head of the beach has changing rooms, showers, WCs and lockers.

THE SOUTH COAST

AROUND MASPALOMAS

5 FINCA MONTECRISTO
7km / 10 mins north of Maspalomas via the GC 504

A botanical paradise: exotic plants from all over the world grow up the steep cliff, with works of art (wind chimes, warriors, giants) peeking out here and there.

Halfway up is a garden restaurant *(booking required | €€€)* serving modern Mediterranean cuisine – you won't find a more romantic spot to dine anywhere on the island. Please note that the location is unsuitable for children because there are no fences along the drop. *Sat/Sun 10am–6pm | admission 8 euros | Barranco de Ayagaures 85 | GC 504, Km5.6 | tel. 928 14 40 32 | montecristo-grancanaria.com | E7*

INSIDER TIP: Secret garden

6 PALMITOS PARK ★
12km / 20 mins north of Maspalomas

In the best leisure park on Gran Canaria, you and your children will not only be able to admire the great variety of subtropical flora but also all kinds of animals. By the entrance is an enclosure with charming meerkats; later you come across gigantic monitor lizards and Australian

Maspalomas offers fun for all ages

MELONERAS

wallabies. There are dozens of exotic birds – mainly parrots, but also flamingos, pelicans, emus, toucans, owls and hummingbirds – in the huge aviaries, some of which you can enter. The bird-of-prey show *(daily 11.45am and 2.30pm)* is fascinating. Lar gibbons and orang-utans live on an island at the bottom of the valley. There is also a butterfly and orchid house, a cactus garden and a large tropical aquarium.

Marine mammals perform their tricks in the Dolphinarium *(daily 1pm and 4pm)*, and other animal shows also provide entertainment *(parrots daily 10.30am, 11.30am, 2.30pm, 3.30pm and 4.30pm)*, while cafeterias and restaurants (€€€) take care of all your creature comforts. The entire park is extremely well cared for. *Daily 10am–5pm | admission 29 euros, 3-4 year-olds 11 euros, 5-10 year-olds 20.50 euros | Barranco de Palmitos | shuttle buses nos. 45 and 70 | palmitospark.es | ⊞ E7*

MELONERAS

(⊞ E8) **Gran Canaria's newest resort has a touch of luxury with its palatial four- and five-star hotels, upmarket boutiques and a promenade along the cliffs with fantastic views that leads to a light-sand beach 400m long.**

Adjacent are the greens of Meloneras' 18-hole golf course.

SIGHTSEEING

There are no classic sights as such, but the Africa-themed *Hotel Baobab* is worth seeing with its fortress-like, ochre-coloured architecture and the baobab trees in the huge pool area. The *Hotel Villa del Conde* has the feel of a picture-postcard Canarian village. It even has a church – have a look inside! *(both hotels at: lopesan.com)* Compared to the hotels, the tiny archaeological area by the promenade, which has a few foundations of round buildings behind an iron fence, appears a little neglected.

EATING & DRINKING

Attractive restaurants ranging from Italian to Chinese are lined up along the promenade.

MAXIMILIAN'S
Time just flies here! The elegant establishment (terrace) serves fine Mediterranean cuisine. Carnivores will love it: try the beef fillet with gorgonzola or mushroom sauce. *Daily noon–midnight | Blvd Faro | tel. 928 14 70 34 | maximiliansrestaurant.es | €€*

PINGÜINO SOUL
This restaurant on the promenade satisfies your needs from morning until night: first there are ice creams, cakes and waffles; then it's light snacks; and from early evening you can enjoy cocktails in a cool ambience. *Daily 9am–11pm | Paseo Meloneras/C/ Mar Mediterráneo | tel. 928 14 21 81 | FB: pinguinosoul | €–€€*

THE SOUTH COAST

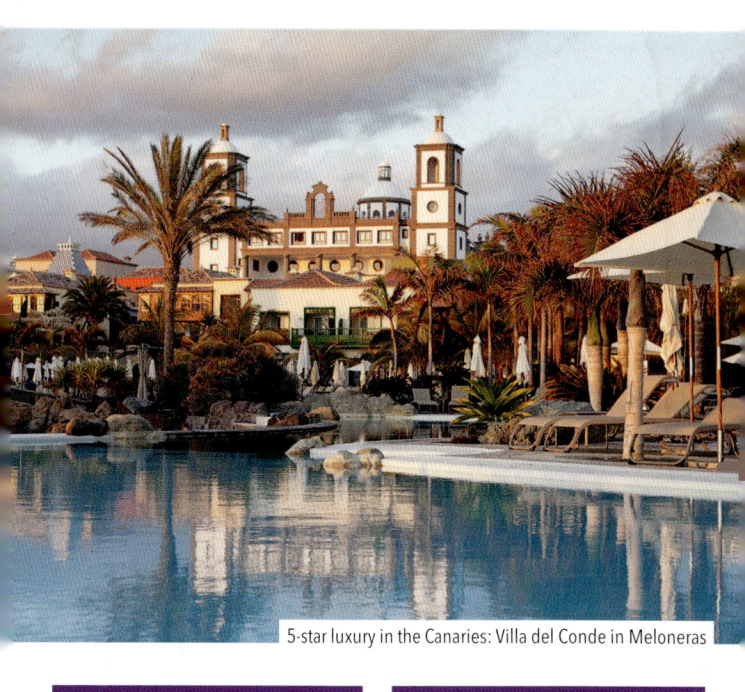

5-star luxury in the Canaries: Villa del Conde in Meloneras

SHOPPING

You can find all that your heart desires in the *Varadero* shopping centre: from clothes, cosmetics and jewellery to groceries, but bargain goods are the main draw. By contrast, the arcade at the hotel *Costa Meloneras* near the beach has a splendid range of top-brand boutiques with expensive high-quality items. If you are looking for a culinary souvenir, then pop in to the *Boulevard Oasis* shopping arcade at *Compañía de la Galleta*: it sells home-made biscuits in typical Canarian flavours such as *gofio*, mango and cactus fruit – all beautifully wrapped, of course.

BEACHES

Although the 400-m-long *Playa de Mujeres* at the western end of the promenade is not as beautiful as the beach of Playa del Inglés/Maspalomas, it's always an option for (sun)bathing.

WELLNESS

GRAN SPA CORALLIUM

In the spa centre of the *Hotel Costa Meloneras* you can enjoy the atmosphere of a luxurious Roman bath with a *caldarium* and *frigidarium* (warm and cold baths), hamam, ice grotto and a "light-and-dream room" where you can lie on a gurgling waterbed and look up at twinkling stars while listening to the music of the spheres.

ARGUINEGUÍN

The highlight is the "Dead Sea": a spacious artificial grotto with extremely salty water in which you can float weightlessly. *Daily 11am–7pm | C/ Mar Mediterráneo 1 | tel. 928 12 81 81 | lopesan.com*

NIGHTLIFE

For some stylish chilling on the promenade, head to the *Café del Mar (daily until 2am | cafedelmarmeloneras.com)*, and then enjoy one of the fabulous dance shows – from Flamenco to Burlesque – that take place every evening.

INSIDER TIP: Ibiza-style

Entertainment at the *ExpoMeloneras (C/ Príncipe de Asturias | expomeloneras.com)*, the large modern building a little inland, is a bit more classical. If you need an adrenalin boost, roulette is played and the slot machines spin tirelessly at the *Casino (casinolaspalmas.com | daily 10–4am, gaming room from 8pm)*.

ARGUINEGUÍN

(*D8*) In the language of the Guanches, the town is called "still waters", a reference to its location in a wind-protected bay. The settlement has a population of 12,000 people, and the same number again of tourists.

Even though Arguineguín, like the neighbouring resorts, is notable for its tourism, you can still experience normal Canarian everyday life here. One

An excursion in a glass-bottom boat is a must

THE SOUTH COAST

of the main sites of activities is the harbour area. It's where the docks are; where old men go to the club room to play cards, and where fish are processed and sold in the warehouse.

The *Líneas Salmón* (see p. 109) excursion boats dock here to unload the day-trippers. There's also a little beach. Above it a palm-lined promenade runs along to the neighbouring beach of Playa de la Lajilla where you can also swim.

EATING & DRINKING

BAR PLAYA EL BOYA 🐷 🚩

At the eastern edge of Arguineguín, next to the cement works, this is the place to go for a filling meal on a budget. Octavio and his crew serve paella and fresh seafood at a fast pace – and at a price that won't be beaten. *Closed Thu | C/ Santa Agueda 32 (El Pajar) | tel. 928 73 53 14 | €*

COFRADÍA DE PESCADORES

At the harbour near the large warehouse where the fishermen prepare and sell their catch, you will find the "Fishermen's Brotherhood". The seafood served here is guaranteed to be fresh. *Closed Mon | tel. 928 15 09 63 | €€*

SHOPPING

Tuesday is market day at the end of the village towards Playa del Inglés – and it's heaving. You can get almost anything here, including crafts and Canarian culinary delights *(Tue 8am–2pm)*.

SPORT & ACTIVITIES

BOAT TRIPS

Feel the sea breeze in your hair while sailing along the coast of Gran Canaria on a relaxed boat tour between Arguineguín, Playa de la Verga, Puerto Rico and Puerto de Mogán. The scheduled boats of ⭐ *Líneas Salmón (daily 10am-4.30pm | return ticket 8–12 euros | ⏱ 30 mins to Puerto de Mogán | lineassalmon.es)*, and the glass-bottom boats of *Líneas Blue Bird (daily 10.15am–5.15pm | return ticket 12–19 euros | ⏱ 30–70 mins | de. lineasbluebird.com)* sail along the coast. You will pass built-up gorges and wild and rugged cliffs on the endless blue ocean …

BEACHES

Backed by low cliffs, *Playa de las Marañuelas* is well-suited for bathing.

AROUND ARGUINEGUÍN

7 PLAYA DE LA VERGA 🌴
3km / 5 mins northwest of Arguineguín via the GC 500

A property tycoon who wanted to improve the marketing of his exclusive resort had Caribbean sand shipped in and created a white beach lined with palm trees. And, since all of Spain's beaches are public, so is this one – as is the yacht harbour and the island of *Maroa* across a bridge. Every

PUERTO RICO

hour, small shuttle boats depart from the pier for other coastal destinations *(see p. 109, boat trips)*.

If you choose to stay put, you can chill out at *Maroa (bar-café daily 10.30am–7pm, lounge bar until 2am)* or play a round of minigolf on the adjacent course *(daily 9.30am–9.30pm | 6 euros)*. *C–D8*

8 BARRANCO DE ARGUINEGUÍN ★

22km / 40 mins north of Arguineguín via the GC 505

The GC-505 leads up into the rugged mountains of the *cumbre*. When you reach an altitude of almost 900m, you can visit the *Embalse de Soria*, the biggest reservoir in Gran Canaria. It's a good place to have a long break (see p. 86). *D5–8*

PUERTO RICO

(C7) **Wherever you look – along both sides of the bay and up the steep cliffs – there are apartments and hotels!**

Puerto Rico ("rich harbour") has long since spilt over into the adjacent valleys. It is especially popular with the British and Scandinavians who enjoy the wind-free location with guaranteed sun and the tremendous

A touch of the Caribbean: Playa de la Verga near Arguineguín

THE SOUTH COAST

range of water sports and other activities. It is also the starting point for many boat trips.

EATING & DRINKING

DON QUIJOTE
The friendly unhurried atmosphere and above-average quality of the food make Don Quijote stand out from the mass of restaurants. They specialise in fish and meat dishes. *Closed Sun and Mon | Puerto Base Edificio Porto Novo | tel. 928 56 09 01 | €€€*

SPORT & ACTIVITIES

ANGRY BIRDS ACTIVITY PARK
Inspired by the popular video game, this activity park in Puerto Rico features water slides and inflatable bouncy castles, trampolines, climbing walls and bumper cars. *Daily 10am–10pm | admission 15 euros, children and groups of more than 3 people 11.50 euros, children under 4 free | Av. de la Cornisa 1 | tel. 928 15 39 76 | activityparkcanarias.com*

AQUANAUTS DIVE CENTRE
They offer the entire range of diving activities, including night dives, when you can experience the nocturnal underwater world. *Puerto Base | Local 5 | tel. 928 56 06 55 | aquanauts-divecenter.com*

BOAT TRIPS
Every morning, around 10am, boat tours leave from *Puerto Base* harbour (at the eastern edge of Puerto Rico). You can choose between pirate trips and sport fishing to catamaran sailing (tickets available on site). With a little luck, you'll spot a pod of dolphins. The scheduled boats of *Líneas Salmón* and *Blue Bird* (see p. 109) depart from *Puerto Escala* harbour further to the west.

INSIDER TIP: Coastal sailing trip with a bonus

BEACHES

The fine, light-coloured sand of the 300-m-long *Playa de Puerto Rico* is protected by breakwaters. Sadly, it is much too small for the many holidaymakers. You can go parasailing, ride a jet ski or hire a paddle boat.

NIGHTLIFE

Whether you want a sundowner with tapas or a proper meal, *Oscar's Pub* on the promenade is the place to go. The youngish crowd lets its hair down after midnight. The most popular disco pubs at the moment are: *Bora Bora, Snoopy, Piccadilly Music Pub* and *Harley'* (scpuertorico.com).

AROUND PUERTO RICO

9 PLAYA DE AMADORES
2km / 3 mins northwest of Puerto Rico via the GC 500

A 15-minute walk along a fantastic ★ *coastal promenade* with magnificent sea views connects Puerto Rico with

PUERTO DE MOGÁN

Playa de Amadores. The 400-m beach is shingle and shell sand. Harbour walls protect it from high waves, making it quite safe for children to swim here. There are car parks, sunbeds to rent and excellent sanitary facilities, as well as many shops, ice cream parlours and restaurants. This is rounded off with a lovely 👶 minigolf course, playground and the *Amadores Beach Club (open daily | tel. 928 56 00 56 | amadoresbeachclub.com | €€)* at the northern end. When the sun goes down behind Tenerife, you can relax on soft cushions, gazing out across the evening sea …

If you want to pamper yourself, visit the 💆 *Talasoterapia Canarias* in the *Hotel Gloria Palace Amadores (C/ La Palma 2 | tel. 928 12 85 28 | gloriapalaceth.com)* where hydro-jets massage you from head to toe in a warm 36°C saltwater basin. The treatments in the adjoining spa range from Ayurveda to Zen. *C7*

🔟 TAURO

3km / 4 mins northwest of Puerto Rico via the GC 500

This town has also been given a tourist makeover. A man-made white-sand beach has been created, and a marina will follow soon. Inland, the *Anfi-Club*, which lets out accommodation on a time-sharing basis, has an eye-catching 18-hole golf course. *C7*

1️⃣1️⃣ PLAYA DEL CURA

4km / 6 mins northwest of Puerto Rico via the GC 500

The narrow, 300-m-long sandy beach with a small promenade is no longer a peaceful experience. The slopes are packed with apartment buildings, but you can still jump into the sea. *C7*

PUERTO DE MOGÁN

(B–C7) **A picture book idyll: narrow lanes with exotic flowering plants, walkways above the water, and a harbour with yachts gently rocking in the crystal-clear sea. Sometimes, so many visitors pass through ⭐ Puerto de Mogán (pop. approx. 1,000 plus 3,000 guest beds) that you'd think it was about to burst at the seams.**

At the end of the 1980s, a pretty holiday resort in the Andalusian-Venetian style was built in a semi-circle in front of the former fishing village in the bay. It had white, flat-roofed houses, narrow lanes and canals into the sea. It also needed a beach. The large marina attracts sailors from all over the world. Fishing boats, the small shipyard and warehouses were cleverly integrated in the harbour.

The old village itself scrambles picturesquely up the cliffs to the north. It's less idyllic at the bottom of Puerto de Mogán's valley. There has been much building here, and it is now crowded with lots of shops, shopping centres and hotels. If you're looking for peace and quiet, then don't come on a Friday, when the whole place turns into a bustling open-air market.

THE SOUTH COAST

SIGHTSEEING

CAÑADA DE LOS GATOS

Opposite, on a south-facing slope, hidden in a rock fissure at the mouth of the *Barranco de Mogán*, are the reasonably well-preserved ruins of an ancient Canarian village. Follow the well laid-out paths past the remains of the settlement and graves, up to the lookout point, which also has a café. The views are magnificent. *Tue–Sun 10am–5pm, in summer until 6pm | café 10am–2pm | admission 4 euros, combined ticket with other archaeological sites 10 euros | C/ La Puntilla | arqueologiacanaria.com | ⏱ 30 mins*

EATING & DRINKING

LOS GUAYRES

Alexis Álvarez, one of the top Gran Canarian chefs, makes traditional Canarian dishes more sophisticated by adding an international touch. Try the six-course taster menu! There are marvellous seats on the terrace. *Closed Mon | C/ la Puntilla 29 | tel. 928 72 41 00 | losguayres.com | booking required | €€€*

INSIDER TIP — Tradition meets avant garde

QUÉ TAL

Everybody in Norway knows the television chef Stena Petterson. His small temple to culinary expertise where he prepares subtle slow-food menus every evening is a great experience. We recommend that you book in advance because the few tables fill up quickly. *Closed Sun | El Paseo de mis Padres 34 | tel. 928 15 14 88 | €€€*

ZONA VERDE

This garden restaurant slightly off the beaten track is Stéphane's atmospheric oasis. He cooks large portions of marinated meat on an open grill, served with home-made barbecue sauces. The smoked swordfish carpaccio is exquisite and, if you manage to save space for dessert, the

Paradise? Playa de Amadores

PUERTO DE MOGÁN

Evening atmosphere on the promenade of Puerto de Mogán

home-made ginger-and-vanilla ice cream with mango is a dream. *Open daily | C/ La Cruz, opposite the bus terminal | tel. 617 02 67 09 | FB: Zona Verde Mogan | €€*

SHOPPING

MERCADO
Things become quite chaotic in Puerto de Mogán on Fridays when tourists from all over the south flock to the market *(9am–2pm)*, despite the fact that there's nothing particularly special about it: a lot of kitsch, commerce and hardly any genuine crafts.

SPORT & ACTIVITIES

BOAT TRIPS
In summer, catamaran excursions (from 50 euros) take you to the beaches of 🏖 Güigüi Grande and Güigüi Chico (see p. 76). Tours by scheduled boat services (see p. 109) are cheaper.

SUBMARINE ADVENTURE 🏖
This 40-minute adventure starts at the pier and leads you deep down 20m to an artificial reef. Provided that there is little swell, you can see shoals of fish and the remains of a wreck. *Daily 10am–5pm, book on site or online | 31.50 euros, children aged 2-12 16 euros | C/ Explanada del Castillete | tel. 928 56 51 08 | atlantidasubmarine. com | free shuttle from the resorts in the south can also be booked at: short. travel/gra7*

BEACHES

The beach of Puerto de Mogán (loungers, showers) is protected by breakwaters. While it is pretty to look

THE SOUTH COAST

at, there is far too little space for all the tourists.

NIGHTLIFE

A sunset stroll is about as exciting as evening's gets in Puerto de Mogán. The harbour and plaza are meeting places for both local people and holidaymakers. You can get well-mixed cocktails with a harbour view at the *Sol & Luna (daily 9.30am–11pm | at the harbour | FB: Sol y luna – Puerto Mogán)*.

AROUND PUERTO DE MOGÁN

12 TAURITO
5km / 10 mins southeast of Puerto de Mogán via the GC 500

Along the shore is a 250-m dark-sand beach. Stretching inland from here is

WHERE TO STAY ON THE SOUTH COAST

HIP HOTEL
The *Hotel Nayra (46 rooms | C/ Irlanda 25 | tel. 928 09 37 11 | hotelnayra.com | €€)* has got a new look: it now resembles a light and bright spaceship that has landed in Playa del Inglés not far from the *Centro Comercial Yumbo*. While appearing smooth and impenetrable from the outside, the interior is spacious, light and welcoming – an oasis of peace which will allow you to relax. If only more hotels in the South were styled like this one …

Lago Taurito, a 2,000-m2 seawater swimming and leisure park with slides, waterfalls and special pools for toddlers *(daily 10am–6pm | admission 17 euros, children 5 euros | in the Taurito resort | lagotaurito.es)*. Hotels and apartments sprawl up both sides of the valley. *C7*

Lago Taurito

DISCOVERY TOURS

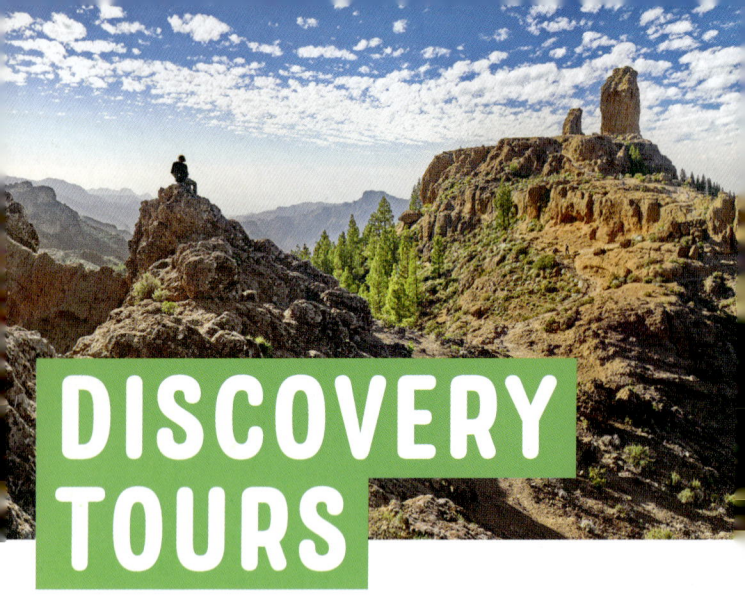

Want to get under the skin of the region? Then our discovery tours are the ideal guide – they provide advice on which sights to visit, tips on where to stop for that perfect holiday snap, a choice of the best places to eat and drink, and suggestions for fun activities..

❶ IN THE SHADOW OF THE "SNOWY PEAK"

- ➤ Far-reaching views, fortress mountains and a gigantic caldera
- ➤ Experience the Guayadeque gorge caves
- ➤ Finally at the *faro* – view the coastline from the lighthouse

📍 Playa del Inglés

🏁 Playa del Inglés

🔄 132km

🚗 1 day (3–4 hrs total driving time)

ℹ️ What to take: swimwear and provisions
Please note: in ❶ **Playa del Inglés**, signs pointing to Fataga are hard to find. Follow the central Avenida de Tirajana northbound until you get to the GC 60.

Breathe high-altitude air at the Roque Nublo

THE EARLY BIRD …

It is worth getting an early start for this tour. From ❶ **Playa del Inglés** ➤ p. 98 *drive through San Fernando towards Fataga*. As soon as you are on the GC 60, the splendour of the mountains will appear before you. Stop at the viewing platform ❷ **Degollada de las Yeguas** and look down deep into the rugged gorge. The next stop is ❸ **Fataga** ➤ p. 88. Wander through this picturesque village in the southern mountains with its small white houses nestled within lush green vegetation.

BEAUTIFUL SPOTS & BIG ROCKS

The road then winds up to ❹ **San Bartolomé de Tirajana** ➤ p. 87. Stop near the church so that you can take a look at the prettily restored **Casa Yánez** ➤ p. 87. This ethnological museum, including a historical doctor's surgery, shows what life was like in the olden days. A few miles after the town, make sure you *turn right onto the narrow GC 654*. Hardly any tourists find their way here, and yet it is one of the prettiest places on the southern side of the island. Small stone houses, surrounded by palm and almond trees, crouch below

❶ **Playa del Inglés**

9km 21mins

❷ **Degollada de las Yeguas**

9km 4mins

❸ **Fataga**

8km 7mins

❹ **San Bartolomé de Tirajana**

mighty rock faces. You can enjoy the views of the Caldera de Tirajana, a rugged crater formed by erosion, with the sea in the distance. Later, you will drive along the foot of the Risco Blanco, a luminous and weathered, giant rock outcrop.

13km 14mins

HAVE FUN WITH THE ANIMALS

In Taidía, the next hamlet, watch out for the (subtle) signs to the ❺ **Donkey Finca Burro Safari Las Tirajanas** *(daily 10am–4pm | from 10 euros/pers | El Morisco | tel. 928 18 05 87 | burrosafari. com).* Almost everything served here is grown on the finca, which practises organic farming methods although it is not officially certified. In the shade beneath a pergola covered in vines, you can enjoy fresh goat cheese, spicy marinated olives and wrinkled potatoes with fiery *mojo* sauces. Children, in particular, will have fun on the half-hour donkey ride along the mule tracks leading into the mountains.

❺ Donkey Finca Burro Safari Las Tirajanas

2km 2mins

INSIDER TIP
Eat with a clean conscience

Fataga is one of the destinations on the winding trip into the mountains

DISCOVERY TOURS

A VIEWPOINT BY THE FORTRESS MOUNTAIN

The sleepy village of ❻ Santa Lucía ➤ p. 88 is also worth a stop. Take a look at the domed, mosque-like church and walk through the lanes above the thoroughfare. Below the village is the gigantic ❼ La Fortaleza Grande. During the Spanish conquest in 1483, the last of the Canarian warriors had barricaded themselves inside the walls of the fortress. *From the GC 65, take the road (4km southwest of Santa Lucía) leading to the car park at the foot of the fortress hill.* If you're sure-footed, you can climb up a few metres to a large cave. Cross over to the opening, which lets light through from the other side, and you will come across a path cut through the rock that will bring you back down to the car park in a few minutes.

❻ Santa Lucía
5km   5mins
❼ La Fortaleza Grande
1km   1min

TAKE A BREAK TO TAKE IN THE VIEW

From there, you should take a little detour (signposted) to the viewing platform ❽ Mirador de Sorrueda high above the glistening reservoir of Presa de la Sorrueda (also called Embalse de Tirajana) encircled by palm trees – stop for a moment and take in the austere countryside all around you. A little further along the road, the ❾ Centro de Interpretación la Fortaleza ➤ p. 89 will give you a vivid description of the final days of the indigenous Canarians. Next door is the El Alpendre *(closed Mon | tel. 675 97 15 44 | €–€€).* This restaurant full of old craftsmen's tools, which resembles a museum, serves freshly pressed juice and wonderful grilled meats.

INSIDER TIP: How about some sustenance?

❽ Mirador de Sorrueda
1.5km   1min
❾ Centro de Interpretación la Fortaleza
11km   17mins

STROLL THROUGH THE OLD BISHOP'S TOWN

Afterwards, *drive back in the direction of Santa Lucía and turn right to switch over to the GC 550.* The narrow and winding road passes weathered mountainsides worn away by wind and water. You will come across the picturesque village of ❿ Temisas that sprawls across a wide mountain spur. On the terraces are hundreds of olive trees whose fruits are harvested to make excellent olive oil.

❿ Temisas
10km   10mins

⓫ Agüimes

4km　3mins

⓫ Barranco de Guayadeque

450m　1min

⓭ Museo de Sitio Guayadeque

3km　3mins

A WALK IN THE OLD TOWN

The road then curves down through sun-basked mountain slopes to ⓫ Agüimes ➤ p. 90. The historic centre with its cobbled streets, all of which lead to the Iglesia de San Sebastián, is worth exploring. Don't miss out on the Museo de la Historia *(Tue–Sun 9am–5pm | admission 3 euros | C/ Juan Alvarado y Saz 42)* where you can learn about everyday life in the past – including witchcraft.

COUNTLESS CAVES

After so much culture, it's time to get back to nature! The ⓬ Barranco de Guayadeque ➤ p. 91, which you can access behind Agüimes (follow the signs!), is a gorge flanked by high rock walls. It is green all year round thanks to several springs. *The road winds along*, past colossal agaves, spurges and huge ferns. The small rustic picnic spots under eucalyptus trees are perfect for a short break. Then head to the ⓭ Museo de Sitio Guayadeque *(Tue–Sat 9am–5pm, Sun 10am–3pm | admission 2.50 euros)* which is built into the rock like a cave. Archaeologists have discovered many pre-Hispanic caves in the Barranco de

DISCOVERY TOURS

Guayadeque in which the indigenous Canarians lived or buried their dead. Some of the artefacts are displayed in the museum.

You should also stop in the hamlet of ⓮ **Cuevas Bermejas** where you can climb up the steep face punctured with holes on step paths leading up from the rock chapel. A few kilometres uphill, almost at the end of the dead-end road, is the labyrinthine *Tagoror* restaurant. From here, another well-marked, 1-km path leads around the ⓯ **Montaña de las Tierras**, offering wonderful views of the valley.

⓮ **Cuevas Bermejas**
4km 4mins
⓯ **Montaña de las Tierras**

YOUR REWARD: SEA & GOOD FOOD

Drive *back to Agüimes and join the GC 100 to head straight to the coast* at ⓰ **Arinaga** ➤ **p. 90**. Although you might be put off by the commercial zone on your way into town, there is an attractive seafront promenade. Have a swim in the ocean if you feel like it. Then follow the coast for a few hundred metres

19km 24mins
⓰ **Arinaga**
33km 32mins

Museo de Sitio Guayadeque explores indigenous Canarian culture

outside town to the Faro de Arinaga *(daily from noon | tel. 928 17 20 31 | €€€)* which can be seen from afar. This historic lighthouse offers fabulous views and excellent food on the cliff. From here, *take the GC 1 to return to the south coast and to* ① Playa del Inglés ➤ p. 98.

❶ Playa del Inglés

❷ THROUGH THE WILD *CUMBRE*

- ➤ Pass the monk to get to the cloud rock
- ➤ Spot a snow well, snowy peak and plunging gorges
- ➤ Round hairpin bends to the bathing spots

◉ Playa del Inglés   🏁 Playa del Inglés

↻ 170km (of which 7km are on foot)   🚗 1 day (5–6 hrs total driving time)

ⓘ What to take: swimwear, warm rainproof clothing, sturdy shoes and drinking water as well as a picnic (you will be able to buy provisions en route in the mountain village of Tejeda).
Please note: at ❸ **Roque Nublo:** you should avoid being out in the hot period around midday!
If the car park at Roque Nublo is full, park 400m further uphill on a plateau.

OVER THE PEAK & INTO THE VALLEY

❶ Playa del Inglés

25km 25mins

❷ San Bartolomé de Tirajana

As with the other tours, make sure you get an early start! From ❶ Playa del Inglés ➤ p. 98 drive to ❷ San Bartolomé de Tirajana ➤ p. 87. the same as for Tour 1. This mountain village is at a height of about 900m. The vertical walls of the *cumbre* will rise in front of you. Shortly past the Cruz Grande rock passage, you will reach the highest point, at 1,260m. *This mountain pass will bring you to the next valley basin.* In the distance, you can see the water of the

DISCOVERY TOURS

well-filled reservoir of *Embalse de Chira* ▶ p. 88 shimmering in the sun.

A ROCKY LANDMARK

Not long after, the hamlet of *Ayacata* ▶ p. 85 will appear among the many almond trees. In January and February, the scent of the blossom fills the air. *In Ayacata, switch over to the* GC 600, which leads to the car park *La Goleta* (Km 11.2) at ❸ *Roque Nublo* ▶ p. 85. The size and appearance of the 80-m-high monolith seems to change depending on where you stand.

28km 46mins

❸ Roque Nublo

CLOSE TO THE CLOUD ROCK

If you want to take a close-up look, follow the marked path (round trip: 4.8km, approx. two hours, height difference of 230m each for the ascent and descent). For this gentle walk, which has only two fairly short, steep climbs, *take the middle path from the La Goleta stone plateau (marked "S 70 Roque Nublo")*. After 800m at *El Fraile* ("The Monk") *keep to the right (towards La Culata)* and start the trail around the Roque Nublo anti-clockwise. After 700m, ignore the fork to the right to La Culata and *walk straight on*. At the end of the broad bend, you will come face-to-face with the rugged Tejeda basin – a truly amazing panorama.

The trail continues at about the same height to a fork (Hoyetas del Nublo). Follow the signs for *La Goleta* to the left. Afterwards, you'll probably break out in a sweat on the 15-minute climb to the *Las Palomas* pass. From here, turn left and follow the path cut through the rocks to the foot of Roque Nublo – the views in all directions are spectacular. On the way back, return to the *Las Palomas* pass and *keep to the left. At the fork after another 300m, keep right:* this rather easy trail will bring you back to the start of the hike.

INSIDER TIP
Like a bird in the sky

YOU CAN'T GET ANY HIGHER

Back in the car, drive through pine forests and past fruit plantations to the *Cueva Grande crossroads where you should turn right towards Pico de las Nieves (GC 130)*. At 1,949m, "Snowy Peak" is the highest point on the island. In December and January, it really does snow here from time to time. At the crossroads between GC 130 and GC 135, take a look at the historic ❹ **Pozo de las Nieves** ("Snow Well"). Snow was once stored here and pressed into blocks so that donkeys could transport it to Las Palmas where it was used for cooling purposes, for example in the hospital. *Continue to the right – stay along the fence of the military listening station – to the highest viewing platform on the island.* Stop for a while and

12km 8mins

❹ Pozo de las Nieves

550m 1min

DISCOVERY TOURS

take in the fantastic view from ❺ **Pico de las Nieves** ➤ p. 83. To the south, the countryside is rough and rocky, but to the north and west, you will see thick forest.

❺ Pico de las Nieves

9km 9mins

VIEWS OF RUGGED GIANTS

Return to the crossroads at Cueva Grande and then *drive straight on (GC 150)* down to ❻ **Cruz de Tejeda** ➤ p. 82, a tourist enclave in an otherwise dreamy setting. You can buy all kinds of souvenirs here and ask questions at the information hut. From the terrace (open to all) of the flagship state-run **Parador**, you can enjoy the particularly fine view of the Caldera de Tejeda. *The road downhill to Tejeda (GC 15) heads through avenues of eucalyptus trees;* every now and then, the Roque Bentayga (1,412m) peeks through the trees. At an altitude of 1,050m, ❼ **Tejeda** ➤ p. 83 is the most picturesque town on Gran Canaria, with lovely streets, squares and the church in the centre. Apart from the fabulous views of the mountains, you'll also find a relaxed ambience, fresh cuisine and great service at the

❻ Cruz de Tejeda

6km 8mins

❼ Tejeda

From the island's highest point the views reach as far as Tenerife

5km 5mins	Casa de Los Camineros ➤ p. 83. If you have a sweet tooth, go to the Dulcería Nublo Tejeda ➤ p. 84 to buy almond treats for a picnic at the Embalse Cueva de las Niñas (reservoir). ==If you prefer savoury food, walk a bit further to the small supermarket and buy some regional cheese *(queso de la cumbre).*==

> **INSIDER TIP**
> **A hearty picnic**

IN THE FOOTSTEPS OF THE GUANCHE PEOPLE

Continue south on the GC 60. After about 4.5km, turn right to ❽ **Roque Bentayga** ➤ p. 85. You can learn about the rock's significance for the indigenous people at the small but attractive **Centro de Interpretación Roque Bentayga** (see p. 85). A hiking trail climbs uphill from the visitor centre (approx. 45-minute round-trip), at first at an easy pace, then a little steeper. The last stretch, which you should avoid if you are scared of heights, leads over stone steps to the place where the ancient Canarians made their sacrifices; it's a magnificent site! You can see the grooves and holes carved into the rocks where they offered their libations to the gods. The rock faces are still dotted with cave dwellings, including the impressive **Cueva del Rey** (King's Cave).

❽ Roque Bentayga

24km 20mins

Tejeda is a good place to buy some of the region's culinary products

DISCOVERY TOURS

PICNIC BY THE LAKE

After your return to the visitor centre, *follow the GC 60 to Ayacata*. Shortly before you reach Ayacata, *make a sharp right onto the GC 605 to the* ❾ Embalse Cueva de las Niñas ➤ p. 86. You can get a feel for the isolated atmosphere of the Canarian mountains on this less travelled road. The "Maidens' Cave Reservoir" is the loveliest reservoir on Gran Canaria and its shores are the perfect place for a picnic.

BACK TO THE COAST

The last stretch of the tour is adventurous. The steep road into the bountiful valley of ❿ Barranco de Mogán ➤ p. 76 requires adept driving skills. ⓫ Mogán ➤ p. 76 is a pleasant, seemingly sleepy village with a few restaurants. The drive back to the coast leads through a lovely valley which, at the end of March, is covered in the heavy scent of orange blossoms. Pass through Puerto de Mogán ➤ p. 112 to get to the old coastal road with its splendid views and to the sheltered bay of ⓬ Playa de Amadores ➤ p. 111. Here you can jump into the water to cool off at the end of the day's tour. *The coastal road GC 500 hugs the sea on the way back to* ❶ Playa del Inglés.

❾ Embalse Cueva de las Niñas
12km 11mins
❿ Barranco de Mogán
5km 5mins
⓫ Mogán
21km 22mins
⓬ Playa de Amadores
22km 23mins
❶ Playa del Inglés

❸ A DAY IN THE GREEN NORTH

- Dragon trees, *gofio* and the Virgin of the Pine
- Picture-postcard towns
- Green terraced fields and black calderas

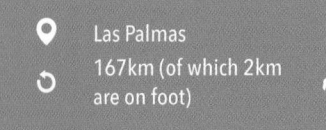

📍 Las Palmas
🏁 Las Palmas
↻ 167km (of which 2km are on foot)
🚗 1 day (7 hrs total driving time)

ℹ️ What to take: warm clothing (possibly rain protection) for the mountains, sturdy shoes for walking, and a picnic
Please note: if you are approaching from the Costa Canaria, join the tour at ❺ **Cruz de Tejeda** (driving time from Playa del Inglés to Cruz de Tejeda approx. 2 hrs). On Sundays: when there is a big market in ❼ **Teror**, the roads are likely to be jammed, so it's better to park outside town.
To visit ❽ **Finca de Osorio:** you need to book online in advance: (cabildo.grancanaria.com/osorio).

❶ Las Palmas
9km 15mins

❷ Jardín Canario
7km 7mins

❸ Santa Brígida
7km 7mins

❹ Vega de San Mateo
13km 12mins

BECOME A BOTANIST

Start the tour in the island's capital. From ❶ Las Palmas ➤ p. 38 take *the GC 110 inland*. Stop for the first break in Tafira Alta where you can visit the ❷ Jardín Canario ➤ p. 53, Spain's biggest botanic gardens. Enjoy a lovely stroll through this botanist's paradise and learn all about the indigenous Canarian flora.

WONDERFUL MOUNTAIN SCENERY

Other good places to stop are the hilltop towns of ❸ Santa Brígida ➤ p. 60 and ❹ Vega de San Mateo ➤ p. 61, whose historic ambience has been preserved around the parish churches.

DISCOVERY TOURS

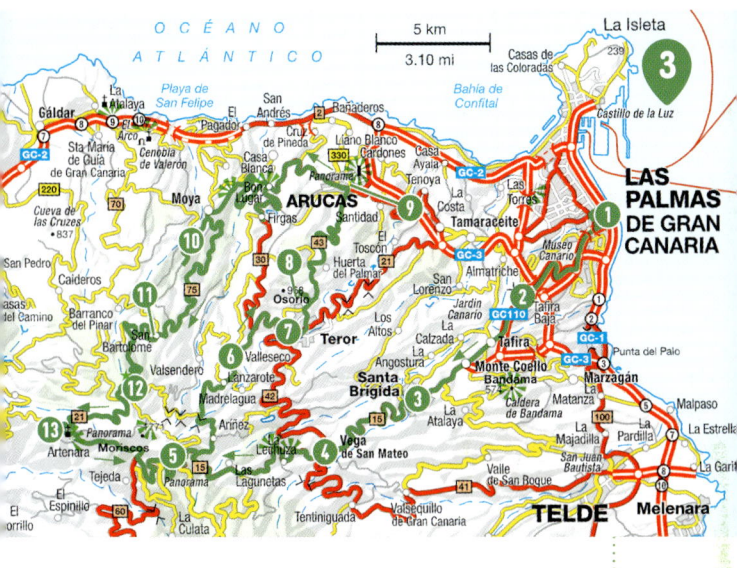

Follow the bends of the GC 15 up to ❺ **Cruz de Tejeda** ➤ p. 82 Gran Canaria's highest mountain pass with a view over the rugged Caldera de Tejeda far below. *Continue towards Valleseco*. The road curves softly down through the green, terraced mountainsides to ❻ **Valleseco**. A tourist information centre is hidden behind the church. Also there is the **Museo Etnográfico** *(Mon-Fri 9am-3pm, Sat 11am-7pm, Sun 11am-3pm | admission free | C/ Párroco José Hernández Acosta 11 | vallesecogran canaria.com)* where you can learn how grain is turned into *gofio*, the Canarian national dish.

TIME FOR A COFFEE BREAK
After some narrow hairpin curves, you will come to ❼ **Teror** ➤ p. 62. Stroll through its pretty squares and streets before you sit down on the terrace of the café **Tasca el Encuentro** *(Tue-Sun 9am-7pm | Plaza 7 | €)* with a view of the pilgrimage church. *Afterwards, take the GC 43 towards Arucas*. After about 2km, stop at the car park in front of an iron gate on the left-hand side of the street. Tour the beautiful residence of ❽ **Finca de Osorio** and stroll through the romantic avenues in

❺ Cruz de Tejeda

10km 10mins

❻ Valleseco

8km 9mins

❼ Teror

4km 3mins

❽ Finca de Osorio

9km 9mins

⑨ Arucas

the large park. You will need to save a bit of time for the next stop. In ⑨ Arucas ➤ p. 64, it is fun to walk past all the elegant mansions.

A CIRCULAR TRAIL IN THE FOREST RESERVE

Pass through Firgas ➤ p. 65 to get to Moya ➤ p. 66, a pretty, small town that lives from farming. *Follow the GC 700 towards Guía, and after 2.5km, take a detour to the laurel forest reserve* ⑩ Parque Natural Los Tilos ➤ p. 66. You can park your car on the right-hand side of the street in front of the information centre *Casa de los Tilos*. The walk around the park takes about an hour (2km).

25km 23mins

⑩ Parque Natural Los Tilos

At the back of the information centre, follow the signs for the nature trail *(sendero del bosque)* – if the wooden gate is closed, you can just ignore it! *Cross over the wooden bridge to get to the little forest*, which is a first step in the attempt to reforest the laurel woodland. After a few minutes, *the path leads close to the street that you need to cross (at house no. 16)*. You will now head uphill, past a resting area and a cave. From atop a rock ledge, you can look over the entire valley. *After 400m, keep left at the fork* and you will soon find yourself back to the information centre.

13km 8mins

FROM THE MIRADOR TO THE CAVE MUSEUM

After your walk, *drive back towards Moya, but then turn onto the GC 75 to* ⑪ Fontanales ➤ p. 66. Are you hungry? At Sibora ➤ p. 66, Señora Fátima serves generous portions of good, plain Canarian food and freshly squeezed juice. After you have eaten, take the *GC 21 towards Artenara*. You will drive past lush green meadows as the road winds

⑪ Fontanales

8km 8mins

INSIDER TIP
Papaya or orange juice?

DISCOVERY TOURS

The old town of Arucas is worth a stop

higher and higher – from the viewing platform ⓬ **Mirador Pinos de Gáldar**, you can look across the entire northern side of the island. After a few miles, you will arrive in ⓭ **Artenara** ➤ p. 79 – with amazing views and the obligatory tunnel walk to the restaurant **Mesón Mirador La Cilla** ➤ p. 81. After a cup of coffee, head to the **Museo de las Casas Cuevas** ➤ p. 79, which exhibits authentically decorated living quarters. *The panoramic GC 210 road* will take you via **Tejeda** ➤ p. 83 back to **Cruz de Tejeda** ➤ p. 82, which marks the end of the tour through the green north. Return the way you came, passing through Vega de San Mateo and Santa Brígida to get back to ❶ **Las Palmas** ➤ p. 38.

8 km	8 mins
⓬ Mirador Pinos de Gáldar	
7 km	7 mins
⓭ Artenara	
47 km	43 mins
❶ Las Palmas	

GOOD TO KNOW
HOLIDAY BASICS

ARRIVAL

TIME ZONE

There is no time difference between Gran Canaria and the United Kingdom.

GETTING THERE
AIR
The cheapest and most convenient way to reach Gran Canaria from the UK is by taking a charter flight. Several companies offer direct flights to Gran Canaria, with departures often from provincial UK airports. Flying time is four to five hours. The frequency of flights and prices vary considerably depending on the time of year, so it is worth shopping around. Most visitors coming from outside Europe will need to fly to Madrid and then take an internal flight to Las Palmas.

Gando Airport is in the east of the island, about 30 to 60 minutes by car from the tourist resorts. Buses to Las Palmas (no. 60) and Playa del Inglés/Maspalomas (no. 66) depart every 30 or 60 minutes. There is an express bus (no. 91) to Puerto Rico and Playa del Cura every hour and a bus to Puerto de Mogán (no. 1). However, they do not depart from outside the arrival hall but from the bus stop on the motorway (300m from the airport!). A taxi to Maspalomas costs around 45 euros, to Puerto Rico about 60 euros and 70 euros to Puerto de Mogán.

FERRY
From Cádiz in southern Spain, the *Compañía Trasmediterránea/Acciona* operates a car ferry that leaves at 5pm on Tuesdays and arrives in Las Palmas 39 hours later. A single crossing starts

Arucas has banana plantations and sea views

at 150 euros per person (from 313 euros with a cabin), and the price for a car is about 200 euros. If you intend to do this in winter (i.e. peak season), make sure you reserve well in advance – either online *(trasmediterranea.es)* or through a travel agency.

Adapter type C

220 V alternating current. Adapters are needed for UK appliances.

GETTING IN
All arrivals from the UK will be required to show a passport, which must have at least six months' validity and must have been issued during the 10 years immediately before the date of entry. Check any other requirements with your airline before you fly.

WHEN TO GO
In the south, where there is little rain and few clouds, the temperatures in winter range between 19°C and 24°C. In summer, the thermometer can be at 30°C and above for weeks. The temperature is significantly lower in the mountains, and it can get very cold above 500m at night, with biting winds in winter. The water temperature is between 18 and 23°C all year round.

GETTING AROUND

BUS
Regular scheduled bus services provided by *Global* are reliable. For the south of the island buses depart

from the central bus terminal – *Estación de Guaguas* – under the *Parque San Telmo* in Las Palmas. The holiday resorts are connected every 15 to 30 minutes between 7am and 11pm. Buses nos. 30, 50 and 91 are express buses that hardly make any stops on their journey from the south to Las Palmas and back *(timetables are available in tourist offices and the ticket office in Parque San Telmo | tel. 902 38 11 10 | guaguasglobal.com)*. Bus services in the island's centre are less frequent, the connections are sometimes rather complicated and you should expect lengthy waits. If you want to explore Las Palmas, you can buy a 24-hour "Tarjeta Live" for only 5 euros; it is valid for all 44 bus routes.

INSIDER TIP
Day ticket for the capital

CAR HIRE

Car rental companies have offices at the airport, in the holiday resorts and in many hotels. You can hire a small car for as little as 25 euros per day (including comprehensive insurance) on a weekly basis. Well-maintained cars (with no hidden extra costs) are offered by the local company *CICAR* (cicar.com), which has branches at the airport and ferry ports, as well as in the resort towns. You have to be at least 21 years old to hire a car, and a deposit is usually required.

RULES OF THE ROAD

The roads on Gran Canaria are generally good and safe. It's really only in Las Palmas that the traffic can get pretty hectic. The speed limit in built-up areas is 50kmh, 90kmh on country roads and 110kmh on motorways. The drink-drive limit is 0.25mg of breath alcohol per litre, which corresponds to 0.5g of blood alcohol per litre (0.3g for new drivers). This is stricter than the UK. Drivers must always have a yellow hi-vis jacket in the car. Yellow marks on the kerb mean no stopping whatsoever; blue stripes mean there is a charge for parking. Only licensed *grúas* (tow-trucks) are allowed to tow vehicles away.

TAXI

All taxis are licensed and fitted with meters, which must be turned on before every ride. In addition to the price per kilometre (plus the basic charge), there are surcharges for Sundays and public holidays, plus night-time, harbour and airport runs, and for large luggage items. If you want to take a taxi for a day's tour round the island, get a quote first.

TRAVELLING BETWEEN THE ISLANDS

You can get to all the other Canary Islands from Gran Canaria. Ferry companies Fred Olsen *(fredolsen.es)* and Naviera Armas *(navieraarmas.com)* generally charge about the same as flights on the regional airlines Binter *(binternet.com)* and Canary Fly *(canaryfly.es)*.

GOOD TO KNOW

FESTIVALS & EVENTS
ALL YEAR ROUND

FEBRUARY/MARCH
Almendros en Flor (Valsequillo & Tejeda): almond blossom with fiesta.
Carnaval (Las Palmas, Maspalomas and elsewhere: *a week-long fiesta with parades and dancing, lpacarnaval.com*

MARCH/APRIL
Transgrancanaria*:* cross the island on foot from north to south, *transgrancanaria.net*

MAY/JUNE
Maspalomas Gay Pride: annual LGBT event, *gaypridemaspalomas.com*

JULY
Nuestra Señora del Carmen (coastal towns): feast day of Our Lady of Carmen, patron saint of fishermen (16 Jul)
Windsurfing World Cup (Pozo Izquierdo): *pwaworldtour.com*

JULY/AUGUST
Festival Temudas Las Palmas*:* modern dance and contemporary theatre (photo), *lpatemudasfest.com*

★ ***Bajada de la Rama*** (Agaete): pine branches are carried from the mountains to the sea where the water is beaten to plead for rain

SEPTEMBER
Romería Virgen del Pino (Teror): a pilgrimage to the Virgin of the Pine, patron saint of the Canary Isles (8 Sept)
Fiesta del Charco (La Aldea de San Nicolás): the "Pond Festival" dates back to 1766 when the bishop discovered people swimming nude in the village pond (10 Sept)

OCTOBER
La Naval (Las Palmas): the Spaniards' victory over the fleet of Sir Francis Drake in 1595 is celebrated (6 Oct).
Masdanza (Playa del Inglés): international dance festival, *masdanza.com*

NOVEMBER
Walking Festival*:* walk around the island with an expert guide – well organised and a bargain, *grancanaria*

EMERGENCIES

EMBASSIES & CONSULATES
BRITISH CONSULATE
Edificio Cataluña | C/ Luis Morote 6-3 | 35007 Las Palmas de Gran Canaria | tel. 928 26 25 08 | ukinspain.fco.gov.uk/en

CONSULAR AGENCY OF THE U.S.
Edificio ARCA | Los Martínez de Escobar 3, Oficina 7 | 35007 Las Palmas | tel. 928 27 12 59 | es.usembassy.gov/consular-agency-las-palmas

HEALTH
Some people can have difficulties adjusting to the change in climate. However, the greatest risk comes from the strong solar radiation (even if it is cloudy, and also in winter). Avoid drinking tap water. Instead, you can buy in 5-litre and 8-litre bottles of mineral water in all supermarkets. Holidaymakers with a European Health Insurance Card (EHIC) will be treated free of charge in health centres and hospitals associated with the Spanish Seguridad Social, the state social security system. All other visitors must have adequate travel insurance. Make sure you receive a detailed receipt for any treatment received in order to claim a reimbursement when you return home. Pharmacies *(farmacias)*, which you will recognise by the green Maltese cross, are open Mon–Fri 9am–1pm and 4–7pm as well as Sat 9am–1pm. The sign *Farmacia de Guardia* points to the nearest pharmacy with an out-of-hours emergency service.

Some useful addresses of hospitals and emergency clinics include: *Hospital Universitario de Gran Canaria (Dr Negrín Barranco de la Ballena | Las Palmas | tel. 928 45 00 00); Clínica Roca (C/ Buganvilla 1 | San Agustín | tel. 928 76 90 04)*

EMERGENCY SERVICES
Call 112 – for the police, fire brigade and ambulance). This service is also available in English.

ESSENTIALS

AIRPORT INFORMATION
Flight information tel. 902 40 47 04

BANKS & CREDIT CARDS
You can withdraw money from ATMs using your EC card or any of the usual credit cards, but there are sometimes hefty charges. Tip: many British banks have local branches or agreements with Spanish banks. Check before you leave home as you can avoid extra charges if you withdraw your money from them. Bank opening hours vary but most are open Mon–Fri 8.30am–2pm and Sat 8.30am–1pm. Almost all hotels, and many shops, restaurants and petrol stations accept credit cards. Some useful numbers to block lost or stolen credit cards are: Visa *tel. 900 99 1124*; MasterCard *tel. 900 822 756.*

GOOD TO KNOW

BUDGETING	
Taxi	2 euros for each km travelled (plus 3 euros basic charge)
Coffee	from 1.50 euros for a café con leche
Tapas	from 3 euros per tapa
Meal	from 9 euros for a menú del día (three courses including a drink)
Petrol	1.50–1.60 euros for 1 litre super unleaded
Ride	from 12 euros for a camel ride

BEACHES
The most beautiful beaches are along the south coast between Playa del Inglés and Maspalomas. The capital Las Palmas also has a long beach of light sand.

CAMPING
Wild camping is forbidden on Gran Canaria. You can only use the 🐷 free public campsites in the mountains if you have obtained prior permission from the *OIAC (Oficina de Información y Atención al Ciudadano/Edificio Insular 1 | Mon–Fri 8.30am–1pm | C/ Profesor Augustín Millares Carló 18 | Las Palmas | tel. 928 21 92 29 | oiac@ grancanaria.com).* It is possible to camp in splendid isolation at the campsite in the mountain village of *Temisas (Ctra Agüimes–Santa Lucía GC 551 | tel. 928 79 81 49).* Camping *Tasartico (Tasartico | tel. 928 89 47 15)* is another site in the extreme west of the island, miles from anywhere, but close to the sea.

CUSTOMS
The Canary Islands have a special tax status. For this reason there are restrictions on goods you can take home with you. The limits are: 200 cigarettes, 25 cigars or 250g of other tobacco products. 1 litre of spirits and 2 litres of fortified wine (such as sherry or port), sparkling wine or any other drink that is less than 22% volume. In addition you may bring back 1 litre of beer or 4 litres of still wine as well as other goods up to the value of 430 euros (children under 15: 175 euros). Check online before leaving home. For tax and duty on goods brought to the UK from the EU see: *hmrc.gov.uk/ customs/arriving/arrivingeu.htm*

INFORMATION
Tourist information is available at spain.info. There is a tourist information office in the airport's arrival hall *(Mon–Fri 9am–9pm, Sat 9am–5pm | tel. 928 57 41 17 | aeropuerto@ grancanaria.com).* In Las Palmas, you can visit the *Patronato de Turismo (Mon–Fri 8am–6pm, Sat/Sun 10am–2pm | C/ Triana 93/C/ Domingo J Navarro | tel. 928 21 96 00).* All the bigger resorts have their own tourist information offices *(grancanaria.com).*

LANGUAGE
In the larger resorts you will get by without speaking Spanish. However, a

smattering of Spanish will come in very handy in more remote places or on public transport. See p.140 for a few useful words and phrases.

NUDE BATHING

Nude bathing is only common in the central section of the Playa de Maspalomas. The Oböna travel company runs a naturist hotel in Maspalomas *(oboena.de)*.

OPENING HOURS

Shops are usually open from 9/10am until 8pm on weekdays. Many smaller shops close for a siesta (1.30–5pm). On Saturdays most places close at 2pm. Large supermarkets and shopping centres stay open Mon-Sat 9am–9pm. Most of the 24-hour shops are located near the port in Las Palmas.

PHONE & MOBILE PHONE

To dial numbers on Gran Canaria from outside Spain, you need the international country code for Spain, which is 0034, followed by the nine-digit phone number including the area code for Gran Canaria (928). The dialling code for the UK is 0044, for the USA 001. Then you need the local area code (without the initial zero), followed by the phone number. You can use your mobile phone on Gran Canaria without any problems. In order to avoid roaming charges (check with your provider) you might want to buy a Spanish prepaid card and switch out your SIM card.

POST

You can buy stamps *(sellos)* at post offices *(correos)* and in newsagents *(estancos)*. Sending a letter *(carta)* or postcard *(tarjeta postal)* should cost between 1.50 euros and 2 euros. Private postal services may be cheaper than the national service, but they but are not always reliable.

PRICES

The prices you have to pay for services is not much lower than in many other European countries. Theme parks are particularly expensive, with tickets for a family of four easily exceeding 100 euros. Thanks to the low VAT, food – including imported food (which most of it is) – isn't much more expensive on the Canary Islands than in Central Europe. Tobacco goods, perfume and a few non-prescription medicines are cheaper than at home.

PUBLIC HOLIDAYS

1 Jan	Año Nuevo (New Year's Day)
6 Jan	Los Reyes (Epiphany)
March/April	Viernes Santo (Good Friday)
1 May	Día del Trabajo (Labour Day)
30 May	Día de las Islas Canarias (Canary Islands' Day)
May/June	Corpus Christi
25 July	Santiago Apóstol (St James' Day)
15 Aug	Asunción (Assumption)
8 Sept	Día de la Virgen del Pino
12 Oct	Día de la Hispanidad
1 Nov	Todos los Santos
6 Dec	Día de la Constitución
8 Dec	Inmaculada Concepción (Feast of the Immaculate Conception)
25 Dec	Navidad (Christmas)

GOOD TO KNOW

RURAL TOURISM

Turismo rural is designed for people who want to discover the real Gran Canaria, far off the beaten track and unspoilt by the mass tourism on the beaches. Guests can live like the locals in *fincas*, manor houses, country hotels and cave dwellings. This type of accommodation – varying from rustic to comfortable – can be found in many villages and small towns. The accommodation is fully equipped for those who want to self-cater and there's a minimum two-night booking. For a good overview visit the website of the *Asociación Gran Canaria Natural (tel. 928 33 41 75 | grancanarianatural andactive.com)*.

TIPPING

If you are satisfied with the service in a restaurant, round up the bill by about 10%. Hotel cleaning and reception staff also expect a tip, as do coach drivers and guides on organised excursions.

WEATHER IN LAS PALMAS

High season / Low season

	JAN	FEB	MARCH	APRIL	MAY	JUNE	JULY	AUG	SEPT	OCT	NOV	DEC
Daytime temperature	21°	22°	22°	22°	23°	24°	25°	26°	26°	26°	24°	22°
Night-time temperatures	14°	14°	15°	16°	17°	18°	19°	21°	21°	19°	18°	16°
Hours of sunshine per day	6	6	7	8	9	9	9	9	8	7	6	5
Rainy days per month	6	3	3	2	1	1	1	1	1	4	6	6
Sea temperature in °C	19°	18°	18°	18°	19°	20°	21°	22°	23°	23°	21°	20°

WORDS & PHRASES IN SPANISH

SMALLTALK

yes/no/maybe	sí/no/quizás
please Thank you	por favor/gracias
Hello!/Goodbye/Bye	¡Hola!/¡Adiós!/¡Hasta luego!
Good day/evening/night	¡Buenos días!/¡Buenas tardes!/¡Buenas noches!
Excuse me/sorry!	¡Perdona!/¡Perdone!
May I?	¿Puedo …?
Sorry?/Could you repeat?	¿Cómo dice?
My name is …	Me llamo …
What is your name? (formal/informal)	¿Cómo se llama usted?/¿Cómo te llamas?
I am from … the UK/USA/Ireland	Soy de … Alemania/Austria/Suiza
I (don't) like this	Esto (no) me gusta.
I would like … /Do you have …?	Querría …/¿Tiene usted …?

SYMBOLS

EATING & DRINKING

The menu, please!	¡El menú, por favor!
expensive/cheap/price	caro/barato/precio
Could you bring … please?	¿Podría traerme … por favor?
bottle/jug/glass	botella/jarra/vaso
knife/fork/spoon	cuchillo/tenedor/cuchara
salt/pepper/sugar	sal/pimienta/azúcar
vinegar/oil/milk/lemon	vinagre/aceite/leche/limón
cold/too salty/undercooked	frío/demasiado salado/sin hacer
with/without ice/fizz (in water)	con/sin hielo/gas
vegetarian/allergy	vegetariano/vegetariana/alergía
I would like to pay, please	Querría pagar, por favor.
bill/receipt/tip	cuenta/recibo/propina

MISCELLANEOUS

Where is …?/Where are …?	¿Dónde está …? /¿Dónde están …?
What time is it?	¿Qué hora es?
today/tomorrow/yesterday	hoy/mañana/ayer
How much is …?	¿Cuánto cuesta …?
Where can I get internet/WiFi?	¿Dónde encuentro un acceso a internet/wifi?
Help!/Look out!/Be careful!	¡Socorro!/¡Atención!/¡Cuidado!
pharmacy/drug store	farmacia/droguería
broken/it's not working	roto/no funciona
broken down/garage	avería/taller
Can I take photos here?	¿Podría fotografiar aquí?
open/closed/opening hours	abierto/cerrado/horario
entrance/exit	entrada/salida
toilets (women/men)	aseos (señoras/caballeros)
(not) drinking water	agua (no) potable
breakfast/B&B/all inclusive	desayuno/media pensión/pensión completa
car park/multi-storey car park	parking/garaje
I would like to hire …	Querría alquilar …
a car/a bike/a boat	un coche/una bícicleta/un barco
0/1/2/3/4/5/6/7/8/9/10/100/1000	cero/un, uno, una/dos/tres/cuatro/cinco/seis/siete/ocho/nueve/diez/cien, ciento/mil

HOLIDAY VIBES
FOR RELAXATION & CHILLING

FOR BOOKWORMS

📖 FIFTEEN DAYS IN NOVEMBER (2003)
Author José Luis Correa from Las Palmas makes his moody detective hunt criminals on Gran Canaria, and if he meets a dead end, he asks his grandfather in the fishing quarter of La Isleta for advice.

📖 LANDSCAPES OF GRAN CANARIA (2003)
Walking guide Noel Rochford, connoisseur and resident of the Canary Islands, takes readers on a trip round Gran Canaria. This guidebook includes four driving tours, 50 long and short walks and 30 suggestions, such as where to picnic.

📖 A DARKER SKY (2016)
Swedish writer Mari Jungstedt sets her murder mystery amid a group of yoga enthusiasts on Gran Canaria, and the local community of Swedish expats is involved.

📖 THE HISTORY OF THE DISCOVERY AND CONQUEST OF THE CANARY ISLANDS (2005)
Translated from Fray Juan de Abreu Galindo's manuscript found on one of the islands, this contemporary account of the mysterious pre-Spanish Canary Islands provides an interesting insight into the life of the ancient inhabitants.

PLAYLIST

0:58

LOS GOFIONES – GRAN CANARIA
The oldest folk group in the Canary Islands, with castanets and powerful singing voices

ALFREDO KRAUS – ISLAS CANARIAS
The Gran Canaria-born singer is regarded as one of the greatest tenors of all times

MARY SÁNCHEZ – ROQUE NUBLO
The legendary singer gives a passionate musical portrait of "Cloud Mountain"

LAS K-NARIAS – TU INDIFERENCIA
Twin sisters Gara and Loida are enjoying mega reggaeton success

KIKE PERDOMO – AHI VA ESO!
Gran Canaria's best-known jazz musician plays light and swinging music, accompanied by Bill Evans

The holiday soundtrack is available at **Spotify** under **MARCO POLO** Canaries

Or scan the code with the Spotify app

ONLINE

GRANCANARIACULTURA.COM
All events are listed here, from fiestas to heavy metal concerts

MIPLAYADELASCANTERAS.COM
Photographer Tino Armas, who is well known on the island, portrays the Las Palmas city beach using photos and videos

FOTOSDEGRANCANARIA.COM
Gallery featuring almost 20,000 images of the island, sorted by location

SUNTIMER
The app uses GPS to match your precise location and the current UV radiation with your skin type, indicating for how long you can safely stay in the sun

STAR WALK
High up in the mountains, the night sky over Gran Canaria is crystal clear and majestic. Using inbuilt sensors in your mobile to determine your viewing angle, this astronomy app explains the stars overhead

TRAVEL PURSUIT
THE MARCO POLO HOLIDAY QUIZ

Do you know what makes Gran Canaria tick? Test your knowledge of the idiosyncrasies and eccentricities of the island and its people. The answers are at the bottom of the page and can all be found on pages 18–23.

❶ Who invented Canarian wrestling (*Lucha Canaria*)?
a) Portuguese immigrants
b) Former emigrants who returned from America
c) The indigenous people of Gran Canaria

❷ How expensive is the carnival queen's costume?
a) Similar to a mid-range car
b) Similar to a racing bicycle
c) Similar to a family home

❸ How long can a camel manage without water?
a) Three weeks
b) Three days
c) Three hours

❹ Why do many Canarios have Berber forenames?
a) Because the continent of Africa is close by
b) Because the indigenous Canarians descended from Berbers
c) Because there are close bonds between the Canaries and Morocco

❺ What is the Canarian dragon?
a) A legend, similar to that of the Loch Ness monster
b) A figure which appears each year at the carnival
c) A tree species that is specific to the Canaries

Correct answers: 1c, 2a, 3a, 4b, 5c, 6a, 7b, 8a, 9b, 10c

Dragon tree in the Jardín Canario

❻ What does the sand of the Dunas de Maspalomas consist of?
a) Ground corals and shells
b) Ground rock that has been blown across from the Sahara
c) Ground volcanic rock

❼ What do the Canarios mean when they talk of a "donkey's stomach" (*panza del burro*)?
a) A full stomach after a good meal
b) A thick grey layer of clouds
c) A culinary delicacy

❽ For many people, Carnaval is THE fiesta of the year, but what is the word's literal meaning?
a) "Farewell to the flesh"
b) "Festival of the buffalo"
c) "Festival of festivals"

❾ Why are Canarian cave houses comfortable to live in?
a) Because they haven't got any windows that might allow nosy people to peek inside
b) Because they are warm in winter and cool in summer
c) Because people have lived like this for countless generations

❿ What is the traditional "Funeral of the Sardine"?
a) A fishermen's fiesta after a particularly good catch
b) An ancient Canarian ritual held to improve the fishermen's catch
c) The burning of a giant cardboard fish at the end of the carnival

INDEX

Acuario Poema del Mar 10, 46
Acusa 21
Agaete 70, 135
Agüimes 90, 120
Angry Birds Activity Park 10
Aqualand (Maspalomas) 10, 104
Arehucas 9, 65
Arguineguín 11, 108
Arinaga 90, 121
Arteara 19
Artenara 21, 79, 84, 131
Arucas 64, 130
Ayacata 85, 123
Bahía Feliz 98
Barranco de Arguineguín 32, 110
Barranco de Ayagaures 32
Barranco de Guayadeque 21, 91, 120
Barranco de La Aldea 79
Barranco de Mogán 76, 127
Barranco de San Miguel 58
Basílica de Nuestra Señora del Pino 8, 63
Basílica de San Juan Bautista (Telde) 58
CAAM (Centro Atlántico de Arte Moderno) 43
Cactualdea 78
Caldera de Bandama 60
Caldera de Tejeda 83
Caldera de Tirajana 87, 88
Caldera Pinos de Gáldar 81
Calle Real de la Plaza (Teror) 62
Camel Safari 10, 104
Camel Safari Park La Baranda 10, 88
Cañada de los Gatos 113
Casa África 45
Casa Condal 99
Casa de colon 43
Casa de Colón 43
Casa Museo León Y Castillo 59
Casa Museo Pérez Galdós 45
Castillo de la Luz 46
Catedral de Santa Ana (Las Palmas) 9, 42
Cenobio de Valerón 67
Centro Atlántico de Arte Moderno (CAAM) 9
Centro de Interpretación la Fortaleza 119
Centro de Plantas Medicinales 83
Charco de Maspalomas 10
Cruz de Tejeda 82, 125, 129, 131
Cuatro Puertas 59
Cuevas Bermejas 121
Degollada de Becerra 82
Dunas de Maspalomas 20, 103
El Drago, Galdar 68

Embalse Cueva de las Niñas 9, 32, 86, 127
Embalse de Chira 88, 123
Embalse de Soria 11, 86
Ermita de San Antonio Abad 43
Fataga 88, 117
Finca Montecristo 105
Firgas 21, 65
Fontanales 66, 130
Gabinete Literario 44
Gáldar 21, 68
Galería del Patronato 99
Guayadeque 91
Güigüi 77
Iglesia de la Asunción 66
Iglesia de San Juan Bautista (Arucas) 64
Iglesia de San Matías 80
Iglesia de San Sebastián (Agüimes) 90, 120
Iglesia de Santiago De Los Caballeros 69
Ingenio 21, 91
Jardín Canario 11, 53, 128
Jardín De La Marquesa 65
Jinámar 30
La Aldea de San Nicolás 78, 135
La Fortaleza 89
Las Palmas 8, 15, 21, 30, 31, 32, 35, 38, 128, 131, 132, 134, 135
Maspalomas 19, 103, 135
Meloneras 15, 106
Mercado de la Vegueta 50
Mercado del Puerto 50
Mogán 76, 127
Molino de Viento 76
Montaña de Arucas 65
Montaña de las Tierras 121
Moya 66
Mundo Aborigen 102
Museo Antonio Padrón 69
Museo Canario 8, 44
Museo de Historia (Agüimes) 90
Museo de la Historia 120
Museo de las Casas Cuevas 11, 79, 131
Museo de Sitio Guayadeque 91, 120
Museo Diocesano de Arte Sacro 63
Museo Elder 46
Museo Etnográfico 129
Museo Néstor 46
Museo Néstor Álamo 66
Museo y Parque Arqueológico Cueva Pintada 79
Necrópolis de Arteara 88
Palmitos Park 10, 105
Parque de Santa Catalina 9, 46, 51, 53
Parque Doramas 45
Parque Municipal (Arucas) 65
Parque Natural Los Tilos 66, 130

Parque San Telmo 45
Pico de Bandama 60
Pico de las Nieves 16, 22, 83, 125
Pinar de Tamadaba 81
Playa de Amadores 15, 34, 35, 111, 127
Playa de las Burras 96
Playa de las Canteras 35, 51
Playa de las Marañuelas 109
Playa de la Verga 35, 109
Playa del Cura 112
Playa del Pino (Treror) 62
Playa del Inglés 32, 34, 98, 101, 117, 122, 127, 135
Playa de Maspalomas 104
Playa de Melenara 60
Playa de Mujeres 107
Playa de Puerto Rico 111
Playa de San Agustín 96
Playa de Tasarte 76
Playa de Veneguera 76
Plaza del Pino (Treror) 62
Plaza de San Juan (Telde) 58
Plaza de Santa Ana (Las Palmas) 42
Pozo de las Nieves 124
Pozo Izquierdo 35, 98, 135
Pueblo Canario 9, 45
Puerto Base 111
Puerto de La Aldea de San Nicolás 11, 78
Puerto de las Nieves 11, 70
Puerto de Mogán 8, 21, 32, 33, 34, 35, 112, 127
Puerto Rico 33, 35, 110
Roque Bentayga 85, 126
Roque Nublo 84, 85, 123
San Agustín 33, 35, 96
San Bartolomé de Tirajana 87, 117, 122
San Fernando 117
San Francisco (Telde) 58
San Juan (Telde) 58
Santa Brígida 32, 33, 60, 128
Santa Lucía 88, 119
Santa María de Guía 66
Sardina del Norte 69
Sioux City 97
Taurito 115
Tauro 112
Teatro Pérez Galdós 45
Tejeda 83, 125, 131, 135
Telde 58
Temisas 119
Teror 31, 62, 129, 135
Tienda de Arturo 11
Valle de Agaete 71
Valle de Tauro 34
Valleseco 129
Valsequillo 60, 135
Vega de San Mateo 61, 128
Vinoteca San Juan 59
Virgen de la Cuevita 11, 80
Virgen de las Nieves 70

INDEX & CREDITS

WE WANT TO HEAR FROM YOU!

Did you have a great holiday? Is there something on your mind? Whatever it is, let us know! Whether you want to praise the guide, alert us to errors or give us a personal tip – MARCO POLO would be pleased to hear from you. Please contact us by email:

sales@heartwoodpublishing.co.uk

We do everything we can to provide the very latest information for your trip. Nevertheless, despite all of our authors' thorough research, errors can creep in. MARCO POLO does not accept any liability for this.

PICTURE CREDITS

Cover picture: Dunes of Maspalomas (Schapowalow/Fantuz)

Photos: awl-images: N. Farrin (58/59); DuMont picture archive (9, 24/25, 27, 85); R. Freyer (8, 67); I. Kain (147); Getty Images: H. Ross (72/73); huber-images: G. Cozzi (105), O. Fantuz (front outer front inner flap/1, 76/77), S. Lubenow (43, 49), R. Mau (14/15), R. Schmid (10, 50/51, 54/55, 131, 143), J. Wlodarczyk (116/117); laif: Heuer (31), M. Kirchner (32/33), Piepenburg (52), D. Revelle (2/3); Look: S. Lubenow (31, 38/39, 100, J. Richter (22); mauritius images (12/13, 18/19, 58, 70, 97, 125, 126/127); mauritius images/y (26/27, 35, 62, 79, 86/87, 121, 132/133, 135), tz (61), S. Hempel (21), P. Tomlins (109); mauritius images/Alamy/A.J.D. Foto Ltd. (47); mauritius images/Hemis.fr: L. Montico (102/103); mauritius images/ib: Katja Kreder (111); mauritius images/imagebroker (back flap, 144/145), M. Moxter (89), F. er (11, 106); mauritius images/Islandstock/y (44, 82); mauritius images/Prisma: R. van der (118); mautitius images/AVA (90); White Star: mm (80, 92/93, 114); T. P. Widmann (6/7, 28); shutterstock.com images: Cristian Mircea Balate (20), rt Galvin-Oliphant (23), Diaz Ojeda (35), Patryk ider (115).

4th Edition - fully revised and updated 2022
Worldwide Distribution: Heartwood Publishing Ltd, Bath, United Kingdom
www.heartwoodpublishing.co.uk

© MAIRDUMONT GmbH & Co. KG, Ostfildern
Authors: Izabella Gawin, Sven Weniger;
Editor: Christin Ullmann;
Picture editor: Veronika Plajer
Cartography: © MAIRDUMONT, Ostfildern (pp. 36–37, 120, 123, 129, outer wallet, pull-out map); © MAIRDUMONT, Ostfildern, using map data from OpenStreetMap, licence CC-BY-SA 2.0 (pp. 40–41, 56–57, 74–75, 94–95, 99)
Cover design and pull-out map cover design:
bilekjaeger_Kreativagentur with Zukunftswerkstatt, Stuttgart
Page design: Langenstein Communication GmbH, Ludwigsburg;

Heartwood Publishing credits:
Translated from the German by John Owen, Kathleen Becker, Jennifer Walcoff Neuheiser, Suzanne Kirkbright
Editors: Felicity Laughton, Kate Michell, Sophie Blacksell Jones
Prepress: Summerlane Books, Bath
Printed in India

All rights reserved. No part of this book may be reproduced, stored in a retrieval system or transmitted in any form or by any means (electronic, mechanical, photocopying, recording or otherwise) without prior written permission from the publisher.

MARCO POLO AUTHOR
IZABELLA GAWIN

Izabella only planned to spend one winter on the Canary Islands, but she felt so at home in the southern sun that she's been coming back every year – good-bye drizzle, farewell winter gloom! And because she found working on the Canaries as easy as living there, she ended up doing her PhD thesis on the islands and took to writing travel guides.

DOS & DON'TS

HOW TO AVOID SLIP-UPS & BLUNDERS

DON'T CAUSE A BLOCKAGE
In many of the toilets, you will be asked not to put paper down the loo. This is because the pipes in older houses are narrow and easily get blocked. So please put used paper in the bins provided.

DON'T TAKE ANY EXOTIC PLANTS HOME WITH YOU
A calla lily, cactus-like euphorbia or mini dragon tree: occasionally visitors get carried away and start digging up these indigenous plants to take home. However, Canarian plants are subject to special protection and they must not be removed from the islands. Instead, buy a packet of seeds in a flower shop (*jardinería*) – it's easier to pack too.

DON'T SWIM IF THERE'S A RED FLAG
Every year, people drown off the coast of the Canary Islands, and often it's due to carelessness. If the red flag is flying on the beach, you must stay out of the water. Yellow means take care, and if the flag is green you can jump right in – although even then take care not to swim out too far.

DO ASK BEFORE YOU EAT
Bread is part of every meal in Spain and once upon a time it was always free. Today it is often placed on your table … before appearing on your bill. It is a good idea to ask if it is *por cuenta de la casa* ("on the house").

DON'T WEAR FLIP-FLOPS IN THE MOUNTAINS
Holidaymakers often get caught out by freezing temperatures in the *cumbre*. As a rule of thumb, the temperature drops by 1°C for every 100m of altitude. So, take a warm coat and suitable footwear.